# The City Homesteader

## SELF-SUFFICIENCY ON ANY SQUARE FOOTAGE

BY SCOTT MEYER

RUNNING PRESS
PHILADELPHIA · LONDON

9  8  7  6  5  4  3  2  1
Digit on the right indicates the number of this printing

Library of Congress Control Number: 2010925947

ISBN 978-0-7624-4085-6

Cover and interior design by Amanda Richmond
Illustrations by Joel Holland
Edited by Kristen Green Wiewora
Typography: Archer, Neutra, and Ziggurat

Running Press Book Publishers
2300 Chestnut Street
Philadelphia, PA 19103-4371

Visit us on the web!
www.runningpress.com

To my grandparents,
**MARCEL & HANNAH MEYER**,
for showing me that food, fun, and family love
can be found in cherry trees.

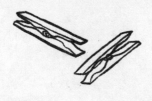

# CONTENTS

# INTRODUCTION

**T**HOSE EARLY HOMESTEADERS must have been the bravest people. Imagine the confidence it took to walk away from civilization and move to the wilderness, where they had to provide everything for themselves. Not even a butcher or baker or candlestick maker to rely on: just the whole family pitching in to reap, make, or use what they needed from the land. Those folks were both determined and resourceful.

Nowadays, our food is produced and processed, packaged and shipped, and often even cooked for us. We live in climate-controlled rooms and are surrounded by stores offering us everything we need, and too much we don't. We spend our days—and more and more of our spare time—connecting to other people and gathering information remotely, even while we live closer to each other than ever before.

And yet the urge for self-sufficiency is a powerful force in the human DNA. Across the country, in city neighborhoods, suburban developments, and small towns, people are once again catching the homesteading spirit. They're not pulling out of civilization and moving back to the land, but they are producing their own food, storing it for the off-season, rediscovering the old ways of keeping house, and raising animals for a purpose, with little or even no land of their own.

Homesteading today is a step out of the virtual world we live in most of the time and into an authentic experience. It's a way to connect with the seasons, the weather, and the natural world outside our windows while getting your hands dirty and producing something real and essential. Grow even a little of your own food and you begin to appreciate the hard work and knowledge of people who do it for a living, and you can't help feeling reverence for the bounty around you. Deal with your own kitchen and yard waste and you take more control of your own little corner of the world. Be more aware of how you use your resources and you see how small steps you take on your own can add up to a meaningful difference for the whole planet.

City homesteading is not about living without indoor plumbing and modern appliances, but it is about knowing you could if you had to—at least for a while. The world around us can seem so out of control and while we can't change that, taking care of your own basic needs can give you a strong sense of competence that's not easy to come by these days.

The pioneers took along with them a few supplies and all the know-how that had been passed down to them from the generations that came before them. For today's homesteaders, it's knowledge and experience that are in short supply. With this book, you have the knowledge of countless modern homesteaders and many of our predecessors right in your hands. From my own experience and from that of many other experts, I've gathered practical ideas you can use right away for living more resourcefully wherever you make your home. I've made sure you have the specifics you need to get started doing it along with hints on ways to get better if you already are.

Within the limited space of one book, though, I can't give you everything now known about gardening, foraging, preserving food, raising animals and caring for your home more self-sufficiently. Whole books have been written on each of those topics. Instead, I've focused in this book on strategies for doing each of those things while living in a city or suburb—not where you have acres of land to work. I realize that you might not be able or ready to fully commit to every aspect of the homesteading lifestyle, but I am sure that even if you try only one skill, you'll feel the great satisfaction that comes with gaining competency. I predict that soon you will want to try and know more.

One of the greatest rewards of trying to live more resourcefully is that the learning never ends, no matter how much you know, you continue to find more and better ways to be self-sufficient. That's been one of the great rewards for me of working on this book. I have been an organic gardener for more than twenty years, but I picked up some new ideas as I researched this book. And while I had a lot of familiarity with the topics in this book, the experts I spoke to and the references I consulted taught me over and over how much I still have to learn.

This kind of know-how is no longer systematically passed along from one generation to the next. We are all indebted to those people who have kept it alive, and in particular to the new pioneers who are homesteading in cities, suburbs, and small towns and sharing their discoveries with a virtual community through blogs and forums. Personally, I am thankful for the countless homesteaders and gardeners who have taken the time through the years to share their knowledge and experience with me.

While we're on the subject of thanks here, I also must express gratitude to a few people who helped with this book. Running Press publisher Christopher Navratil tops the list for his encouragement and guidance in developing the book's idea. All that a writer can ask for in an editor is a thoughtful reader with enthusiasm for the topic, smart ideas, and dedication to quality. I so much appreciate that Kristen Green Wiewora has been all that and more. I can never thank Buz and Janet Teacher enough for their friendship and support. Finally, and yet always first and foremost, I must thank my dear wife Dawn, whose love and understanding are the most precious resources I know.

# CHAPTER ONE:
# GROWING YOUR OWN

**S**upermarkets today are packed with more food in a greater variety than our grandparents ever imagined possible. You can buy every kind of vegetable and fruit year-round, not only frozen and canned, but shipped in fresh from all over the world. While just a few generations ago, growing food at home was a necessity for most families, vegetable gardening had started to become the quaint hobby of a relatively few aficionados.

And then came news reports of fresh produce tainted with toxic pesticides and potentially lethal bacteria. News about climate change prompted many to begin calculating their carbon footprint and "food miles," the long distances their meals traveled before reaching their plate and the resulting environmental impact. More and more people began to recognize that they had lost touch with where their food came from and that it had become nothing more than fuel for their busy lives, that they were out of sync with the seasons and nature.

Now, the generation raised on food from a bag or box is rediscovering the simple pleasure of producing some of their own food and sharing it with others. Not just people with acres to farm and experience raising crops, but anyone with the desire and nothing more than a small backyard, balcony, or sunny windowsill to grow a few food plants.

You can be a part of this revolution of new food producers. Wherever you live, no matter how much room you have for a garden—or even if you have none at all—you can reap the soul-satisfying rewards of picking the freshest, safest, most healthful food possible. You can grow and eat homegrown food just about all year long. In this chapter I'll take you through the basics of raising your own food, and I'll share strategies, techniques, and tricks for getting the most food from whatever space you have to work with.

# The Right Site

**If you have any spot that gets just a** few hours of sun each day where you can dig into the soil, you can grow a food garden. By choosing crops that produce an abundant yield and using your space efficiently, you can harvest your own fresh vegetables, fruit, and herbs from spring to fall in most climates. With a few low-cost aids, you can even extend your growing season into the cold months.

Before you decide on where to plant your garden, take the time to observe it at different times of day and, if at all possible, over several months. The most productive gardens get eight or more hours of direct sunlight during the height of summer—this is what master gardeners and plant tags mean when they refer to "full sun." If the spot you choose gets less than eight hours of sunlight ("partial sun" or "partial shade"), your choices of what to grow will be a little more limited, but you can still grow a lot of your own food. Plots that get fewer than four hours of direct sun each day, known as "full shade", are not well-suited to growing food.

In **full sun** you can grow all of the most popular garden crops, including tomatoes, strawberries, peppers, peas and beans, cucumbers, squash, melons, corn, and raspberries.

In **partial shade** you won't get a robust harvest of "fruiting crops," like those I listed for full sun, but you can still grow a lot of leafy vegetables, such as lettuce and spinach, as well as root crops like carrots and beets and herbs such as basil and rosemary.

**Full shade**—beneath a tree or in the shadow of a tall building—means you'll need to implement Plan B: container gardening.

The other critical factor in choosing where to site your garden plot is drainage, or how much water the soil holds. You want to avoid spots where water stays in puddles for more than a few hours after a heavy rainstorm, because most plants drown (yes, drown for lack of air) in standing water. But you also don't want it to drain away too quickly—before plants' roots can absorb it—which is often the case where the soil is predominantly sandy. To assess the drainage where you want to plant your garden, try this easy test:

1. Dig a hole that's about the size of a one-gallon milk jug.

2. Fill the hole with water.

3. Check the hole an hour later. If it's empty, the soil drains fast. If there's still water in the hole, check it again after two more hours pass.

4. If the water has drained away between two and four hours after you poured it into the hole, you have ideal drainage (and probably soil that is nice loam, which is the highly desirable balance of clay, sand, and silt).

5. If the water takes more than four hours to drain, this is not an ideal spot for a garden.

1.

2.

3.

You can improve the drainage of your soil if it is slow, but where water stays in puddles for days after a rainstorm, you will be continually combating its natural tendencies. For that reason, low-lying areas and other spots where rainwater collects are not suitable for gardens. The ideal spot for your garden is at the top of a slope (so water naturally drains away) that's facing south or west (the directions that get the most sun in summer).

No matter how much space you have, I strongly suggest you start with a small garden the first season. A single bed or two about four feet wide and eight to ten feet long is big enough to produce a steady supply of different vegetables and herbs from spring to fall. Many new gardeners are very ambitious in spring, plant a big garden, and then become frustrated or disappointed when they can't keep up with it as summer arrives. So I say, start modestly and add more in future seasons once you have a clearer idea of the garden's demands and your capacity to care for it.

# RAISED BED SOLUTION

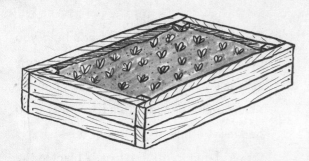

**If the soil where you want to grow** just won't drain well, is full of clay, or otherwise is too adverse to planting, you can solve the problem by building a raised bed. Actually, raised beds make gardening better in almost every situation. A raised bed is just an area where the soil is mounded above ground level: you control the quality of the soil. This lets you give your plants room for the roots to spread out. Raised beds drain water efficiently and the soil warms up more quickly in the spring than the ground does, extending your growing season. And you can build raised beds right on top of a lawn.

• *The perfect width.* A raised bed can be any length that fits your available space, but make it no wider than four feet. You want to be able to reach into its center comfortably from any side without stepping into the bed. Walking on your garden soil compacts it, or squeezes all the air out of it, making it hard for roots to grow.

• *Above the ground.* To get all of the benefits of a raised bed, the top of the soil mound needs to be at least six inches above ground level. Higher is even better, though taller than eighteen inches is unnecessary.

• *Frame the bed.* Raised beds don't have to be framed; the simplest are mounds created by digging out and piling up the soil from the areas around the beds. But mounded beds erode in winter when roots aren't holding them together, so you may need to rebuild them every spring.

The easiest way to make a raised bed, specially on top of grass, is to build a basic frame. You can use stone, bricks, or any kind of lumber, but avoid railroad ties oozing creosote or any other kind of treated wood. Those chemicals can leach into the soil where you are growing food. Even easier, look online and in stores for raised kits that assemble as easy as kids' toys. No law says the bed has to be rectangular—a neighbor of mine has a circular raised bed (the frame is made from chicken wire) in a small sunny spot in her front yard where she grows salad greens in spring and fall. Make sure the bed is more or less level for even drainage.

• *Fill the bed.* After the frame is in place, fill it with a well-blended mix of equal parts compost, peat, and topsoil. This will give your plants the ideal nutrients for growth, disperse moisture evenly and, if it's at least six inches deep, smother grass or most anything else growing beneath it. It's essentially weed-free gardening.

• *Plants in place.* Raised beds help you break loose from the dull row-beside-row garden layout. You can plant in any pattern that you like—or none at all. To plant a raised bed most efficiently, think of the space in terms of quadrants. Each has a plant at the corners and, depending on the plants, maybe one in the center.

*More beds.* If you have room for more than a couple raised beds, try to leave at least three feet between them. That will give you room to bring a wheelbarrow or garden cart right to the beds. Each season, top off all the beds with more compost.

# High-Yield Crops

**When you're trying to get the most** food from a limited space, you want to grow plants that really pump out the produce efficiently. As you're planning your garden, consider these options:

## FOR THE TINIEST SPACES

*Beets* are a real two-for-one because you eat the greens on top (they're tender enough for salad and sturdy enough for sautéing) and the roots that form below ground.

*Cherry tomatoes* are the most productive type of tomatoes, yielding sweet little red fruit by the thousands.

*Leaf lettuce* is sometimes known as "cut-and-come-again" lettuce because you plant it once and snip the leaves as you need them. Let a few leaves remain on the plant when you harvest, and new ones will soon replace the ones you took. Heading lettuce, by contrast, produces one head, and then the harvest is over.

*Pole beans* need only a small space to root in and then pump out pints of crunchy pods almost daily. The bean harvest can go on for weeks in summer. The pea season isn't as long—they're done when summer heat sets in—but they use space just as efficiently as beans and produce lots of pods as long as the temperatures stay cool.

*Radishes* take just 45 days from seed to ready-to-eat, so they're through in time for you to plant something else in its place. "Succession planting," or growing multiple crops one after another, is one of the most valuable strategies for producing a lot of food from a small space. I'll explain more about succession planting in the next section of this chapter (page 17).

## ONLY FOR LARGER SPACES

*Corn* must have critical mass to get thorough pollination (essential for well-filled ears), which makes it hard to grow enough to produce a substantial harvest. Plus, sweet corn is widely available as a local crop throughout the United States, so it's rarely worth devoting some of your limited garden space to it. If you have the irresistible urge to try (I understand, I've succumbed myself), I suggest you plant one of the miniature popcorn varieties that will leave you with a fun, unique harvest to enjoy when the growing season is over.

*Strawberries* return every year, and when they do, the plants slowly spread throughout your garden space. In a few seasons they colonize so much territory that you won't have much room for any other crop. If you love strawberries (who doesn't?) and have only a small plot to garden, grow them in a pot instead of the ground. (You'll find a plan for a strawberry pot on page 31.)

*Melons*—see pumpkins and squash, which are their close cousins.

*Pumpkins and other squash* don't just spread: they conquer. Small gardens are no place for ground-hogging vines like these.

*Heirloom tomatoes* are delicious, unique, and fun to grow, but most of the older varieties do not produce as much as newer ones. You have to plant more heirloom tomatoes to get the same yield, so they're not an efficient use of your space.

*Head lettuce*, like iceberg or Bibb, give you just one harvest, while leaf varieties give you multiple cuttings.

*Broccoli and cabbage* are in the same category as head lettuce—one-and-done harvests that take up too much of the growing season.

# Succession Planting

**Your most critical challenge if you** want to harvest a steady supply of home-grown food is planning. Yes, planning is more important than digging, planting, watering, and even weeding. Take the time to think through the crops that grow well in different conditions, and your garden will continue to produce food from the start of spring to the end of fall.

Spring starts out cool, so you want to start your season with crops that thrive in lower temperatures, including lettuce, spinach, and other leafy greens, peas, carrots, radishes, beets, and if you have room, broccoli and cabbage. Plant them as early as possible—these all tolerate (and many benefit from) a little frost.

The average last frost date for your area is a valuable bit of information. You may find it online or you can ask your county extension office (every county has one, usually associated with your state's land-grant university). After the last frost date, you want to harvest the last of the cool-weather crops, take out the plants, and replace them with tomatoes, peppers (hot and sweet), green beans, cucumbers, zucchini, and basil, all of which grow best in warm weather.

When the warm season winds down and the first frost of fall nears (you want to know the average first frost date, too), pull out those heat-lovers and plant new rounds of lettuce, spinach, kale, and other cold-weather crops. Again, many of them, such as carrots, benefit from a touch of frost. In fact, while carrots are not the most efficient use of your space in spring, they are a very valuable choice in the fall because you can store them in the ground (right where they are growing) until you're ready to eat them—almost to the start of the following spring.

For years I struggled to grow spinach in the spring. By the time the garden's soil dried out enough for me to work in it and plant the seeds, the temperature quickly became too warm for the spinach, turning the leaves bitter, and the plants began flowering before I harvested enough for more than a salad or two. Then I learned to plant spinach in early September—four or five weeks before the average first fall frost where I live in southeastern Pennsylvania. The seeds come up quickly because the soil is still warm, and the plant thrives in the cool days and nights as summer turns to fall. I get a light harvest of fresh green leaves to eat before the first hard frost comes in mid- to late October and the plant's growth slows. When that happens, I surround the plants with a thick mulch of fall leaves (shredded by my lawn mower) and top them with a light (inch or so) cover of leaves, too. The plants remain alive through winter—even when we have a heavy snowfall—but they're dormant, so there's no new growth. As soon as daytime temperatures climb above 55 degrees F in spring, I clear the mulch off the top of the plants and over a week or two gradually pull it away from the plants. Before long, the plants are growing again and I've got bowls-full of fresh green spinach leaves to enjoy—weeks before spring-planted greens are ready. I've tried this technique with arugula, too, and it works just as well for that hardy green. Growing spinach and arugula over winter is an easy and rewarding way to extend your season.

Consider including garlic in your succession plan, too, because you plant it in your garden in fall, it grows all winter, and it's ready to be harvested the following late spring/early summer—just in time to replace it with another crop like green beans that will grow fast and be ready for harvest before the warm season is over. Garlic not only puts your garden to use when it is otherwise dormant, it produces a lot of food for you from a little space—you plant the cloves and each one yields a whole new head of garlic. A pound of cloves yields about seven to ten pounds of fresh garlic heads. Bonus: you can snip and eat a bit of the chivelike greens that grow above ground while the bulbs are forming below.

The goal of succession planting is to keep your space as productive as possible each month of the growing season. To do that, you want to minimize the amount of time each plant is in the ground until it's ready to harvest. Seeds take time to get established, grow roots, and mature enough to bear fruit or eat. So, whenever possible, transplant seedlings (or even larger plants) you grow yourself or buy at a nursery instead of starting with seeds.

Also, as you choose which varieties of each crop to grow, you'll see that some mature faster than others. The fastest-maturing varieties make the best use of the time you have allotted in each season.

# *Vertical Growing*

**The space you have on the ground** may be limited, but you can still expand the area you have to garden in. Just grow up! By setting up trellises and other structures for plants to climb up or lean against, you move your garden into "airspace."

Tomatoes, peas, beans, cucumbers, zucchini, and other summer squash, even small cantaloupes work well in vertical gardens. When selecting varieties of these crops, read the labels carefully and look for "vining" or "pole" types rather than "bush" types.

You can buy trellises and other plant supports specially designed for each kind of plant. Many resourceful gardeners make them using salvaged materials. One of the most ingenious I've seen was a bed frame stood on end, twine woven from top to bottom and side to side, turned into a sturdy pea net. Fallen tree limbs and branches work and give your garden a natural look.

Even easier to work with and available for a low cost, bamboo poles and zip ties let you design and set up a trellis that's perfect for your garden without tools or even construction skills. Check out "Bamboo Trellis" on the next page to see how to make one for yourself.

# BAMBOO TRELLIS

TRELLIS IS A FANCY-SOUNDING WORD FOR A STRUCTURE YOU SET UP TO GIVE vining plants room to climb. You can make a simple trellis with just three bamboo poles, zip ties (twelve inches or longer), and heavy-duty twine. Thinner, lighter poles work well in tight spaces and with lighter vines, like cherry tomatoes and beans. Get heavier poles for big beefsteak tomatoes, cucumbers, and summer squash. If you have the room, you can line up several of these, anchor them to each other, and double or even triple your vertical growing space.

**1.** *Start with a loop.* Take the pointy end of the zip tie, insert it into the square end, and pull it through just a little, but don't tighten it. You'll hear the "zip" sound as you pull it if you did it right.

**2.** *Gather the poles.* Stand the poles on end and hold them in one hand, but with the bottoms spread out to form a triangle. Slip the zip tie loop around the bamboo poles, slide it down to just above the first ridge in the bamboo, and cinch it tight. Make sure the zip tie stays above the pole's ridge so it stays in place.

**3.** *Spread the legs.* Hold up the poles with one hand and spread the legs with the other. (An assistant makes this easier.) You want the legs two to three feet apart. Balance the trellis so it stands up on its own. Dig holes four to six inches deep for each pole, place the poles in the holes, and then refill with the soil you dug out so that the poles are anchored securely.

**4.** *Weave a web.* Starting at the top, wrap the twine horizontally in a spiral pattern all the way around the outside of the tripod, ending at the bottom. Make a vertical piece to finish the net by looping from top to bottom through the horizontal netting.

**5.** *Plant and guide.* Sow seeds or set transplants around all three sides of the tripod. As the plants start to grow, gently guide them upward—some may start off by sprawling along the ground, but once they're on the twine, they will continue climbing upward themselves.

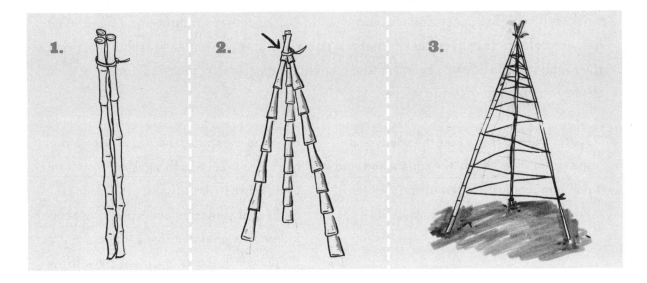

1.

2.

3.

# Edible Landscaping

**When you look around your home**, do you see a bunch of flower beds and no space for a vegetable garden? Who says? Today food plants are showing up in even the finest ornamental beds. Front yards are no longer off limits to vegetables. These are just a few ideas for getting more produce (or any food) from the space you have available to you.

Peppers (hot and sweet) come in a wide array of shapes and sizes, and they ripen to vivid red, orange, or yellow, colors that match those of marigolds and zinnias in late summer. The pepper plants tend to stay small—less than four feet tall—so they look proportional to the flowers.

Rhubarb has brilliant red stems and bright green leaves that complement the daffodils and tulips that come up at the same time.

Match fall-blooming chrysanthemums with edible kales and cabbages, which also thrive in the cool temperatures. Look for varieties of those leafy green vegetables that get purple highlights when the mercury falls.

Thyme, parsley, sage, and other herbs can provide a leafy contrast to all sorts of flowers.

There are no limits to what food and flowering plants you can mix together. When you are considering which to plant, try to site those with similar water needs close to each other—it saves you time and uses water most efficiently.

# Self-Savers

I'll cover how to preserve your own food in another chapter, but while we're still in the garden (or at least that's how I am imagining us), let's discuss crops that, in a sense, preserve themselves.

*Dried beans.* From pinto to kidney, lentils to turtle beans, legumes are high in protein and deliver a lot of nutrients per calories to you. They are all easy to grow in most climates. They do, however, take a long time to mature, occupying their space in your garden for almost all of the growing season. But within that time they not only gather in all those nutrients, they also dry down and are just about ready to be stored. Of all the crops you grow, legumes are the most likely to feed you through the winter.

*Carrots.* As I explained in the section on "Succession Planting" on page 17, carrots can be stored in the ground through the cold season until you want to eat them. If you live where the soil freezes hard, spread a layer of straw or dried grass clippings about a half-inch deep in your carrot bed. The mulch helps keep the soil pliable enough for you to easily pull or dig the carrots out in cold temperatures. Other root crops, such as beets, parsnips, and turnips, can be handled the same way.

*Garlic.* Like a flowering bulb—it is a member of the lily family—it needs to have a chilling period before it will grow. Plant garlic in October, mulch it well (like you do carrots and the other roots crops), and then leave until the following spring. Let the bulbs sit in a cool, dry place away from direct sunlight for a couple weeks after harvest to "cure," and they'll be ready to keep and eat as you need them through to the next season.

*Onions.* Though a close relative of garlic, onions grow during the warm months. But like garlic, if you cure onions after harvest, they will keep for months. Be sure to look for varieties that have been bred for storage, such as Yellow Globe and Corpa.

*Potatoes.* Again, a couple weeks of curing following the harvest and you have home-grown food you can eat as you need it for months. The more starchy types keep better than those with a flakier texture. Sweet potatoes store equally well.

*Sunflowers.* Just a pretty flower, you say? You don't have to be a bird to appreciate the protein-rich seeds and the ease of storing them. After the seeds start to form, cover the head of each sunflower you want to keep with a piece of cheesecloth or other fabric that lets light and water get through. (Be kind: leave a few for the birds, chipmunks, and other hungry critters.) When the stalks start to dry and turn brown, pull the plants, cut off the stalks, and take the heads to a cool, dry, shaded place and remove the cloth. After a couple weeks, rub the seedhead back and forth on your hand or along a screen with openings large enough for the seeds to fall through. Put a bucket or tub underneath to catch the seeds as they fall. Spread them out in a single layer on a tray, and let them dry for another couple weeks. Now they're ready to store or eat.

*Squash.* Varieties with a hard rind and dry flesh, including acorn, butternut, Hubbard, and spaghetti, as well as pumpkins, are all set for storage when you harvest them in late summer or early fall.

Moisture is the only serious threat to storing these self-preserving crops for long periods. Be sure they are completely dry before you stash them away in a spot that is very low in humidity. And make sure that air can circulate around them so that they stay dry. In the food preservation chapter (page 91), you can see how to set up a root cellar in a very small space for storing vegetables over the winter.

## PERENNIAL CROPS

PLANTS THAT COME BACK YEAR AFTER year, even when their aboveground leaves and stems die during winter, are known as perennials. You are probably familiar with some flowering perennials, such as irises, daylilies, and bleeding hearts. There are also a few perennial food plants, and they are very well suited to growing in flower beds, borders alongside buildings and walls, and other places where you can't or don't want to dig up and plant with new crops every year. The group of perennial food plants includes asparagus, chives and some other herbs, horseradish, raspberries, strawberries, and rhubarb. Plant them once, and they will give you a steady harvest for up to twenty years after.

## *Just Herbs*

**If you're not ready to make a com**mitment to growing a whole garden full of food, the simplest and most immediate way to add homegrown flavor to your meals is with herbs. All you need for an herb garden is a spot that gets sun four or more hours of the day and where the soil is very well drained (herbs cannot tolerate sitting in water for even a short period of time). And they give a lot of flavor from the tiniest spaces.

**Basil, cilantro, dill, fennel**, and **parsley** are annuals—you plant them anew each year, although if you don't harvest all of your cilantro, dill, and fennel, they will flower and then bear seeds, which in many areas come up on their own the following year.

**Chives, marjoram, mint, oregano**, and **thyme** are perennials that survive through the winter and continue to come up for years. In regions where winters are not so frigid, rosemary and sage are also perennial. They don't survive most winters in my garden in Pennsylvania, but I've seen shrub-size rosemary plants in northern California that must have been in the same place for ten years or more.

# Containers

**So you live where there is absolutely** no space to plant in the ground or there is too much shade where you can find space. You can still grow plenty of food to eat fresh and store.

Almost every vegetable you want to grow in the ground, you can grow in a pot. Okay, maybe cukes, zukes, and pumpkins are not very practical for containers, but most of the other popular crops, including tomatoes, lettuce, peppers, basil, even strawberries and potatoes, produce well in a pot.

You get the best yields when these crops take in eight hours or more of sunlight each day. One of the benefits of growing in containers is that you can move them during the growing season—or during each day—to spots where they'll get all the sunlight they need.

## CHOOSING A CONTAINER

Plastic, wood, or clay pots all work fine for growing vegetables and herbs. Go for the biggest size you can fit on your deck or balcony, but be sure you can lift it when it is full of soil in case you need to move it. Plastic is lightest in weight. Wood and clay look better and feel more natural, but they dry out faster than plastic, so you have to be more vigilant about watering them.

You can pick up so-called self-watering containers, which have a reservoir space where you add water and then the roots of the plants grow into the water and drink up as they need it. This can be very convenient if you can't check on your containers at least every other day. If you're the forgetful type, check the reservoir of your self-watering containers on the same day every week. If you want to make your own version, all you need are two containers—a larger one without drainage holes and a smaller one with drainage holes that will fit inside it. The plants go in the smaller one and you add water to the larger one. A couple handfuls of gravel in the bottom of the larger pot help to keep the smaller one from sitting in standing water, which can oversaturate some plants.

Your container choices are in no way limited to objects sold as flowerpots. Buckets, barrels and jugs, bathtubs and commodes—whatever your style, you can recycle any salvaged vessel into a cool and functional vegetable planter.

## FILL 'ER UP

The soil you put in your containers is important and can make all the difference in your harvest. Soil you dig up outside is not well suited for growing vegetables in a pot. If it's predominantly clay, then it's too dense for container plants. Sandy soil doesn't provide enough nutrients for the plants.

Bagged potting soil is better, but it can be loaded with synthetic fertilizers (look for the blue or green crystals) and doesn't hold and disperse moisture well. You can make a much better mix yourself. Just blend one part finished compost (homemade or store-bought) with one part peat moss or coir (coconut fiber sold in nurseries). Your plants will get nutrients from the compost, which also holds and disperses moisture steadily. The peat or coir ensures that the mix has enough air pockets and drains well.

## FOOD AND WATER

Unless you're using the self-watering containers, check the moisture in your containers every day or at least every other. Push your finger into the soil until it reaches the second knuckle. If the soil feels damp, no water needed. But if the soil is dry as far down as your fingertip reaches, wet it thoroughly.

The temptation to feed your container plants with "miracle" fertilizers that promise exceptional results is strong, I know. But give me a moment here to explain why that isn't the wisest choice.

First, those synthetic fertilizers are like steroids for plants. They stimulate dramatic, unnatural growth that stresses the plants and burns them out. You are likely to get eye-popping stem and leaf growth, but no more fruit—and maybe even less!—than you would without the fertilizer.

Second, nitrates are a very common element in synthetic fertilizers. They are salts that dehydrate your plants and over time change the pH of your soil. Most vegetable plants grow best in slightly acidic soil; salts turn the soil alkaline.

Third, synthetic fertilizers are made from petroleum by-products, which we all know is not a sustainable resource.

Instead, feed your container plants with fish-and-seaweed fertilizer or compost tea (see page 189). These provide your plants with nutrients in exactly the form they are found in nature. You can also scratch a little compost into the top inch or two of soil in each container.

# HANGING GARDENS

These days you see a lot of advertisements for kits to plant tomatoes in a hanging basket and grow them down instead of up. It's a fun idea that many gardeners (and maybe even more non-gardeners) are trying. It's a nifty solution for growing your own tomatoes where there is no space to plant in the ground. Cherry tomatoes and bush-type larger tomatoes are best for this use.

To try this yourself, simply cut a hole big enough for a tomato stem in the bottom of any hanging flowerpot, then thread the tomato through the hole so that the vine hangs down and the roots are inside the pot. While holding the tomato vine in place, fill the pot with soil, then tamp it down firmly to be sure the plant is in securely. You can plant short-stemmed herbs and flowers, such as thyme or sweet alyssum, on top of the planter.

**Small Space Project**

# STRAWBERRY POT

**Small Space Project**

**PICKING YOUR OWN FRESH STRAWBERRIES IS A GREAT WAY TO START AN EARLY** summer day. In a special planter that will fit anywhere—even on a fire escape—you can harvest a daily supply of juicy and ripe berries for weeks. These pots are designed for the way strawberries grow—with pockets that allow each plant its own space and excellent drainage to keep the roots from staying soggy.

*Pick a perfect pot.* The ideal container is at least twenty-four inches tall, with a wide mouth and six to eight pockets on the sides of the pot. Look for a planter with pockets that have a cupped lip, which prevents soil from spilling out and helps hold in water. You can find these in garden centers and online.

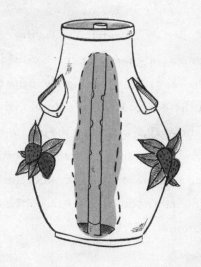

*Choose the right berry.* Strawberries come in two types: "June-bearers," which produce a lot of berries all at once (yes, typically in June) and "everbearers," which give you a steady but smaller harvest of berries from late spring into summer. You want an ever-bearing variety, which are sometimes labeled as "day-neutral," so you never get so many berries you can't keep up with the harvest. Tri-Star and Tribute are two everbearing varieties that work well in a pot.

Another option is alpine strawberries, sometimes called *fraises des bois*, European strawberries, or wood strawberries. They are slightly smaller than the berries we are familiar with in North America, but very intensely flavored. And because the plants and fruit are smaller, they fit nicely into a pot.

*Prep the soil.* In a large bucket or tub, combine two parts sphagnum peat moss or coir (coconut fiber) with one part compost (homemade or bagged). Moisten but don't soak the soil mix. Premoistening keeps the plants from washing out of the pot when you first add water to it. When choosing soil mixes, avoid products that come premixed with synthetic, time-released fertilizer or water-absorbing polymers.

*Insert a tube.* This step isn't essential, but it helps ensure that your strawberries get an even amount of moisture and steady airflow, which make for healthier, more productive plants. Get a piece of PVC pipe that is capped at one end, and cut it to a length that will fit inside the pot with the uncapped end even with the pot's rim. Drill one-eighth-inch holes an inch apart down, alternating sides of the pipe. Some gardeners add gravel or pebbles to the tube to further stabilize it and disperse moisture evenly, but it is not necessary.

*Fill with soil.* Put a few inches of damp soil mix in the bottom of the pot, and then insert the tube, capped end down, into the center of the pot. Holding the tube to keep it centered (or mostly), add the rest of the soil mix around the tube until the pot is nearly full.

*Plant the pots.* Place one plant in each of the pockets. Gently tease the plant's roots apart so they spread out into the soil and then set it in the pocket with the roots angled down. Firmly pack a handful or two of soil mix around them to make sure the roots have solid contact with soil. Continue filling all the pockets with plants, and keep adding soil mix until the container is filled to within a couple inches of its rim. Plant two to three plants at the top.

*Water well.* Keep the soil in the container consistently moist, especially in the first couple weeks after planting. If you put the tube in the center of your pot, pour the water right into it. If not, water the pot from the top slowly to be sure it percolates through the soil and doesn't just run out at the bottom. You may need to water this pot every day during hot, dry spells.

*Feed right.* The slowly released natural nutrients in liquid fish and seaweed fertilizer or compost tea make the healthiest diet for your strawberries. Feed them when they first begin to flower and then once a month for the rest of the season. Be careful not to overfertilize—more is not better—or the plants will quickly become too cramped in the pot and produce too few berries.

*Store for the winter.* In the fall place the pot in a sheltered area where it may get some moisture from snow or rain. In many climates the strawberries will come back again in the spring. If not, you can start over with new plants next season.

## *Variation:* HANGING STRAWBERRY BASKETS

*Suspending strawberries off the ground* is a great way to keep slugs, snails, and sow bugs from ravaging them. Five to six strawberry plants can grow in the top of an ordinary hanging basket. But if you want to make the ultimate hanging strawberry basket, gather twenty-four strawberry plants, a sixteen-inch wire basket, potting soil, and some sphagnum moss, coir, or a basket liner. Line the wire basket with the damp sphagnum moss, coconut fiber, or basket liner. Insert eighteen of the plants into the basket sides through the sphagnum moss. After you have finished, fill the basket with a mix of equal parts peat and compost. Plant the remaining plants in the top of the basket. The basket will continue to produce fruit for about three years if you bring it in each winter.

Place the strawberry pot in a sunny location, and rotate it every few days so that each plant gets enough sunlight. Continue to water the plants every day. Pick the berries when they're ripe and ready to eat, so new ones can grow in their place.

# Small-Space Fruit

**Fruit is the most ideal local food.** It needs no preparation and it's never better than when you pluck it from the tree or vine and take a bite on the spot. Most of us are familiar with the seasons—berries, melons, cherries, peaches, and plums in the summer changing over to apples, pears, and grapes in the fall. Many farms offer you the chance to "pick your own," if you want to get a lot of fruit to preserve. But even without the acreage to plant an orchard, you can enjoy the satisfaction of eating fresh-picked homegrown fruit. You do need to consider, though, that aside from strawberries and melons, fruit growing requires several years to produce a consistent, substantial harvest.

**Strawberries** grow well in a garden bed or even in a container (see page 31 for how to make and use a strawberry pot). If you want a steady supply of a handful of berries that you can pick over several weeks, go with "everbearing" (also known as "day-neutral") varieties. If you're planning to make strawberry jam or pie, choose June-bearing varieties that produce all of their fruit at once. Alpine strawberries are smaller than the more common types, they're intensely flavored, and they're almost never found in supermarkets. After the harvest is over, most strawberry varieties send out runners—or vines that spread along the top of the soil—which set down roots and become new plants that bear berries the following season. If you don't have space for strawberry plants to spread out like that, you can just trim off the runners and start with new plants you buy the next year.

**Raspberries** may be the easiest garden crop you ever grow: Plant them this year, then pick the fruit next year and every season thereafter, with no fertilizing or maintenance or even watering once they're established. They need to be in full sun, but they grow and produce well in even the thinnest, least fertile soil. And raspberries are a great bargain, because in the store they can cost you $3.99 a pound or more. Most experts recommend that you buy "virus-free" stock to plant, which is a sensible idea because raspberries are prone to four widespread diseases that can dampen, or even eliminate altogether, your yields. But if you know a gardener who has healthy raspberries, you can dig up a few fresh shoots from their patch and replant them in your garden. The only care you should give raspberries regularly is to cut down the canes that fruited last season—they won't produce berries again, and cutting them to the ground will stimulate new shoots to grow and keep your patch looking neat.

**Blackberries** and **boysenberries** are equally easy to grow—and even more of a bargain, often priced at $5.99 a pound—but they do pose one challenge if you have limited room. Blackberries and boysenberries spread aggressively after a few years, and a small patch can become a massive thicket if you don't cut them back each year.

**Blueberries** fit into small spaces, but you do need room for at least two plants—one male, one female—to get fruit. The plants are attractive with pretty white flowers in spring and leaves that turn a vivid red in autumn, so you might find a place for them in a bed or border alongside other ornamental shrubs. Blueberries are also more demanding about growing conditions than other berries. They need soil that stays consistently moist and has a low pH (that is, acidic soil). To be sure you get to enjoy more of the berries than birds do, you want to spread protective netting (found in garden centers and online) over the relatively low-growing blueberry shrubs.

**Grapes** need a sunny spot that's at least eight feet long—that's all the space it takes to grow your own sweet and juicy grapes for making jelly, juice, or wine, or eating fresh off the vine. While the seedless green grapes that are a staple in kids' lunchboxes grow well only in California's climate, Concord-type grapes thrive just about every place in North America. They grow on long, woody vines that require support. You can train them onto a fence, an old swing set or clothesline, or any other open, sturdy structure you already have. Or you can set up a simple trellis. That sounds more involved than it is. All you do is get three eight-foot-tall posts and place them about four feet apart. Between them, run two lengths of galvanized wire about three and six feet up the posts. Plant two grapevines in the middle of each section—about two feet from each end—and as they grow, you will guide them to spread their vines along the wire. Fall is the ideal time to plant grapevines. The following autumn you'll have a few bunches of grapes to pick. In just a few years, the vines will bear a heavy crop of sweet fruit. To keep the vines producing and prevent them from becoming a tangled, leaf-heavy mess, they need to be pruned each year. You can find detailed guidelines for pruning in books and online, but basically you want to leave last year's new growth and clip off anything older.

Peaches, plums, apricots, and other stone fruits grow on trees that are relatively short—typically twenty feet tall or less. That makes them a good fit for sunny spots in small yards. With their beautiful and fragrant flowers, you can also use them as an attractive alternative to an ornamental tree in your front yard. Try to place them where they will get morning sun. Wherever you plant them, be sure that air flows freely around them—they are prone to fungal diseases that are minimized when the dew is dried off them early in the day and where breezes can keep them free of excess moisture. Of these three, peaches are the most forgiving, and you can find many varieties selected for tolerance to a wide range of conditions.

Cherries are also a stone fruit that blooms with lovely pink flowers in spring, but they typically grow on trees that get to be forty or more feet tall. If that's too big for your space, you can find dwarf varieties that reach only fifteen or twenty feet tall. Smaller trees are easier to cover with netting to protect the fruit from birds, which is essential if you want a substantial harvest for yourself. Pie (or tart) cherry trees tend to be more tolerant of different soil and climate conditions than sweet cherries are. Both need full sun to produce a full crop of fruit for you.

Apple trees come in dwarf sizes, too, and you have lots of varieties to choose from. But if your space is very limited, consider a "columnar" apple tree. It has a very straight trunk that reaches just eight to ten feet tall and short branches that stop at about two to three feet wide. They produce full-size fruit and often start bearing in their first year, but the yield typically is less than that of a standard or even dwarf tree. A columnar apple tree is small enough to grow in a large (twenty gallon or more) container. Remember that a tree growing in a pot needs to be watered frequently during dry spells and fertilized periodically, because it cannot draw moisture and nutrients out of the soil like a tree planted in the ground can.

Lemon and lime trees adapt very well to life in a pot. The dwarf varieties stay as short as eight to ten feet tall and they can be moved inside during the winter if you don't live where they can survive outside all year—that is, Florida, the Gulf Coast, Arizona, and southern California. In an office building where I worked, a Meyer lemon tree in a pot set beneath a skylight not only survived year-round but bloomed and bore fruit without ever going outside. The fragrance of the flowers was reason enough to walk past it as often as possible.

Figs are another warm-climate fruit that you can grow in a small space with a little extra management. If left in the ground to grow year-round, a fig tree can be as tall as fifty feet high. But where winters are frigid, you need to dig up fig trees each fall and store them inside (wrapped in burlap) until the following spring. This keeps the trees from ever growing much taller than fifteen to twenty feet tall.

## TROPICAL FRUIT FIX

One of my neighbors here in Pennsylvania handles three banana shrubs much the same way I suggest growing fig trees—digging them up in the fall and replanting them in spring. The harvest depends on the weather: In the sweltering summer of 2010, each of the three stems bore one large hand (about six bunches) of ripe bananas, but when the weather is cooler and less humid, he gets less or even no fruit. Still, the plant grows great big leaves every year and is always a topic of conversation among passers-by.

# Going into Overtime

**If you are eager to get growing in** spring, determined to keep your garden producing in fall, or just want to get more of that homegrown food to last all year long, you can extend your gardening season, no matter what the climate is where you live. The techniques you can use to achieve this goal range from simple to serious. Let's start with the most basic and work up to the most involved.

## WINDOWSILL

In a south-facing window, basil, chives, parsley, dill, and rosemary get enough light in winter to stay alive and grow enough for you to snip sprigs steadily.

## COLD FRAME

Simply a box with a transparent, hinged lid that rests on the ground, a cold frame is a kind of "hot box" used to start seedlings before it is warm enough to move them to your garden. You can also use a cold frame to get early and late harvests of cold-tolerant crops like lettuce and other salad greens. Making one is as simple as attaching a salvaged window sash to a box made with four planks. Use a hinge to attach the window so you can open the box on sunny days—direct sunlight through the glass can make it so hot inside that it will roast your plants—and close it when the temperature drops again at night. If you want to go all high-tech, you can buy hinges designed to pop open the lid when the inside temperature reaches a preset point. Here's a simple plan you can use to build your own cold frame.

1. Pick up an old window, from the curb, a barn sale, or a salvage yard. Or call a window contractor and ask if you can have or barter for one of the old windows he replaces. Get the biggest one you can find.

2. Measure the window's height and width.

3. Mark your measurements on a sheet of plywood, then cut it into four pieces matching those sizes in length. The pieces should be at least eighteen inches wide, but if you have the tools and the skills to cut the side pieces on an angle, you can make the cold frame as low as six inches in the front and eighteen inches in back. Angling the cold frame maximizes the amount of direct light the plants inside are exposed to when the sun is low on the horizon.

4. Nail or screw the frame pieces together into a box.

5. Set the window over the box. Attach the window to the back side of the box with hinges and wood screws. You can add a simple hook-and-eye latch in the front, if you want.

6. To make it easy to prop open the window on hot days, use a single screw to attach a small piece of scrap wood to each side of the box. You should be able to swivel these up to hold the window open.

7. Set your cold frame in a sunny location, facing south if possible.

## ROW TUNNEL

Another way to extend your salad harvest into the colder months is to create a protected environment for them right in the garden with knee-high metal arches set up in a row and then wrapped in plastic such as polyethylene, which lets in light and air but helps insulate the plants. I'm no fan of plastic in a garden, but the material used for row tunnels is very durable, so you can use it from year to year, and these tunnels can give you a month or more of additional growing time on either end of the season.

## GREENHOUSES

I'm not here to tell you about glass conservatories or large-scale food production plants. Today, you can find greenhouses as small as a bookshelf or that can fit into your window. Add grow lights to supplement the short days in winter, and for a modest investment, you can harvest just about any vegetable you want in any season.

# NO-SPACE POTATO BARREL

**Small Space Project**

THE DIFFERENCE BETWEEN A HOMEGROWN POTATO AND A STORE-BOUGHT ONE can literally be measured in the moisture lost as the spud makes it way across the country. Freshly dug potatoes are juicy—almost as much as an apple!—and have a meltingly soft texture. You don't need a potato farm in Idaho to discover this for yourself. You can grow a crop of potatoes in any sunny spot that's big enough for an ordinary trash can.

*Start in spring.* Potatoes take all season to fully mature, so begin this project around your average last frost date (which you can find out from your county extension agent).

*Select the spuds.* They grow from chunks of last year's crop—chunks with an "eye," or rootlet, are referred to as "seed potatoes." Each "eye" produces a cluster of new tubers. You can find countless potato varieties in nurseries and online, and you can use any one you want, but small to medium-size ones work best in a barrel. Be sure to get certified disease-free seed potatoes, because they can suffer from nasty problems like scab.

*Pick a barrel.* Plain or fancy, it's your call. Gardening catalogs and Web sites offer barrels specifically designed for growing potatoes. But they are mostly about being more attractive—not functionally better—than one you make at home out of a whiskey barrel or a common trash can. If your container has been used before, be sure to scrub it out well to get rid of fungi that might cause your potatoes to rot before you harvest them.

*Drill for drainage.* If the barrel doesn't already have holes in it where excess water can drain out quickly, drill a few in the bottom and in the sides close to the bottom. Quarter- to half-inch holes are big enough.

*Give it a lift.* Set the barrel in a sunny spot and get it up on blocks or bricks so it sits a few inches above the ground and air can circulate around it.

*Add the soil mix.* Make up a soil mix by blending three parts of compost with two parts of peat moss. Fill the bottom of your barrel six inches deep with the mix. Dampen the mix.

*Plant your spuds.* Place the seed potatoes a couple inches apart in the soil mix. Keep the mix moist but never soggy (which can cause the potatoes to rot).

*Cover after sprouting.* In a week or so the seed potatoes will have sprouts about six to eight inches tall. Add more soil mix to cover them up to their bottom leaves. Again, keep the mix moist, but not soggy. Repeat the process of allowing the sprouts to grow, adding more soil to cover the sprouts and moistening the soil until the barrel is filled to the top.

*Keep the moisture constant.* Remember to keep the soil damp but not wet. Feed the plants with liquid fish and seaweed fertilizer (available at nurseries and home centers) weekly or biweekly until you see little white or yellow flowers on the vines, which indicate that the new potatoes have begun forming.

*Dig for buried treasure.* At the end of the growing season, the vines turn yellow and die back. The potatoes are fully grown. Carefully tip the barrel over, and sift through the soil for the potatoes. Brush the dirt off them (don't wash them until you're ready to cook them), and store them in a cool, dry place away from direct sunlight.

# OPEN SPACES

WHEN YOU REALLY HAVE NO PLACE TO GROW, OUTSIDE OR IN, YOU DON'T HAVE TO give up altogether on the idea of growing your own food. Try one or more of these options.

*Community Gardens.* More than 4,000 empty lots, parks, playgrounds, and other spaces in the United States have been transformed into community gardens, where people in the neighborhood can sign up for plots. Check in with the American Community Gardening Association (at www.communitygarden.org) to find one near you or get information on starting your own.

*Yard-Sharing.* You have the enthusiasm to grow your own food, but no space in which to do it. They have room to plant, but no time or interest in the process. You connect online (at www.craigslist.org or www.yardshare.org) and strike a deal. You plant and care for a garden in their yard and share the harvest with them. Good old-fashioned barter. Just be sure to clearly define the expectations for both parties upfront.

*Guerrilla Gardening.* Abandoned lots, median strips, and lots of other little pockets of potential growing space are just begging for someone to come along and plant them. If other people see you caring for a forgotten space in your neighborhood, you might even inspire a revolution.

# Going Indoors

**Little or no outdoor space for gar-**dening can't prevent you from growing some of your own food. Living in a cold climate with a short growing season is no obstacle either: you can produce food indoors. You don't need a fancy green-house or expensive grow lights to do it. All year long you can grow fresh salad greens and herbs inside your home using a simple setup you can make with mostly recycled materials. You can also raise a steady supply of super-nutritious bean and greens sprouts in your kitchen. With an easy plan on page 48, you can harvest your own gourmet Belgian endive. Your answer is to focus not on what you can't grow, but on what you can.

## WINDOW FARMING

Innovative amateurs have developed a resourceful and fun way to grow vegeta-bles indoors year-round. They're setting up simple hydroponic growing systems using recycled bottles, air pumps from aquariums and plastic tubing, and they're hanging them, like living curtains, in their windows. From a standard four-by-six-foot window, they're harvesting a fresh salad every week.

You can find many different designs for window farms and simple kits for build-ing one at The Windowfarms Project (www.windowfarms.org), a community where users are sharing their experiences and improvements. In the most basic setup, the plants grow in recycled 1.5-liter bottles filled with a liquid nutrient solu-tion (no soil) that is pumped to them from a gallon-size bottle below them. The plant bottles are attached to a rod or dowel using zip ties and set on a windowsill. In the winter months, fluorescent lights sup-plement the shorter daylight hours.

Salad greens and herbs are the easiest crops to grow in a window farm, and probably the most worthwhile, too, since you can cut some to eat and leave the plants to produce more. Most any short-stature crop works well, too. Vining crops like peas and cherry tomatoes need more management—specifically twine or other sturdy support—but they make a fun addition to a window farm.

I'll always believe that the healthiest food grows in soil rather than the unnatural environment of water laced with nutrients—the conditions of a hydroponic setup. But I must admit that the freshness you gain from growing food in your home probably makes up for the diminished nutrient content of food grown hydroponically. And I know a window farm will start conversations about fresh, local food and self-sufficiency that more than compensates for the unnatural arrangement of hydroponics. Let me urge you, though, to always use organic fertilizers rather than synthetic ones. You might not get the eye-popping growth that comes from steroid-like chemical fertilizers, but you also

won't be flushing toxins into the waste stream. You don't want to go to the trouble of growing your own food only to steep it in a soup of ammonium nitrate (the science class name for the main ingredient in most synthetic fertilizers). Go for plant food made with fish and kelp instead. Your window farm may smell a bit like a marsh, but it won't remind you of the lab at a pharmaceutical company.

## ABOUT SPROUTING

Even if you live in a basement apartment, where no daylight ever comes in and the only soil is on the carpet (my brother lived in a cave like that once, and the only thing that grew there was mold), you can raise a crop of homegrown sprouts to add to sandwiches, salads, and stir-fries. You don't need artificial grow lights or any other special equipment. And sprouting is so easy, kids can do it—which they often do at school or with the Scouts. Sprouts come from seeds of many different plants, and they're very healthful because the nutrients in the plant are concentrated. Best of all, you don't even need much patience—sprouts are ready about a week or so after you start them.

## SELECT SEEDS

Every vegetable and grain seed produces a sprout you can eat. They're all equally easy to grow, but their tastes and textures vary a bit. The most popular are alfalfa and mung bean, but you can grow tasty sprouts from broccoli, lentil, radish, dill, buckwheat, and sesame seeds, and many others. Sample a few to find out which you like best.

You can find seeds specifically chosen for sprouting from dedicated suppliers online or catalogs, but regular gardening seeds work, too. Be sure, though, to get organic or at least "untreated" seeds for sprouting. Many commercial seeds are coated with fungicides and other toxic chemicals that you definitely don't want to handle when you're sprouting.

## START THE SEEDS

Sprouting happens when seeds get enough moisture to open or soften their hard exterior and the plant "embryo" inside begins to unfurl. Your job, then, is simple: keep the seeds moist until the sprout emerges and begins to grow. A very basic way to do that: place a handful of seeds on a damp paper towel, fold it in half and then quarters, slip it into a resealable plastic bag, and keep it in your refrigerator. Check it daily and moisten the paper towel if it starts to dry out. After about a week you'll have sprouts ready to eat.

The paper towel method is easy, but you can't grow a lot of sprouts that way. For a steady and more substantial harvest, grow them in a jar. Again, you can buy a specially designed sprouting jar online or via mail order, but an ordinary canning jar or a very thoroughly cleaned mayonnaise jar works well, too.

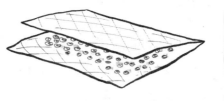

Put a couple tablespoons of seeds into a quart-size jar. You can use more of larger seeds, but be careful not to grow too many seeds in one container or they will become a mildewy mess. Soak the seeds overnight (or about ten to twelve hours) in room-temperature water. Cover the jar with cheesecloth, nylon mesh, or screening. This type of lid lets air circulate in the jar and allows moisture to slowly evaporate. Secure the lid to the jar with a rubber band. After soaking, remove any seeds that are floating—they're duds—and pour out the water. Rinse the seeds in fresh water, and then drain it all away. Be thorough about draining, because you don't want the seeds or little sprouts sitting in water.

### RINSE, REPEAT, RINSE, REPEAT

Keep the jar in a cool place—not the fridge, but the coolest room temperature spot in your home—and away from sunlight. Three times a day, at least twice if that's all you can manage, rinse the seeds and drain the water. (Be even more resourceful by catching the rinse water in a bucket or watering can and using it for watering garden or house plants.) The goal of the rinsing is to keep the seeds damp but not soggy. That's why thorough draining is critical.

### LIGHT OR NOT

Most seeds start to open after four to six days of constant moisture, and you can almost watch the sprouts growing hourly. If you keep them away from direct light, they'll stay mostly white and have a relatively bland flavor. Put the jar where it gets sunlight (or even fluorescent light, if you are sprouting in your office cubicle), and the sprouts develop chlorophyll and a stronger taste. Try sprouting both ways, and you'll know which flavor you prefer.

### HARVEST AND STORAGE

As you're rinsing the sprouts, the seeds' original hulls begin to float free. Remove them, and when they're mostly gone—about eight to ten days after you start the seeds—the sprouts are ready to harvest. You can eat them right away. If you don't, you can store them for a few days in a plastic bag in your refrigerator. By the time you've finished them, your next fresh batch should be just about ready.

## ALL-SEASON ENDIVE

Witloof chicory isn't exactly a popular or even familiar vegetable in North America. It has a leafy green with a texture like curly kale and a slightly bitter taste. At times when coffee has been scarce, its root has been ground and brewed into an acceptable substitute. In northern Europe it's prized as Belgian endive, tangy shoots served raw or in cooked dishes. To modern homesteaders, it is most valuable as a food that you can grow and harvest inside through the winter.

Start by planting witloof chicory seeds in spring, after the last frost. Chicory grows like any other salad green in your garden. You can harvest a few of the early, tender leaves, but as the days grow longer, they taste bitterer. Just leave the plants to continue growing through the summer and into fall, making sure you water deeply during extended dry spells so that it develops a long, deep root.

After a few frosts, but before the ground freezes hard for winter, dig up the long tap roots (which look like a white carrot) and cut the tops off to an inch or two long. Fill large nursery pots or buckets with peat, coir (coconut husk), or coarse sand, and moisten the medium well. Replant the roots into the pots.

Put the buckets in a cool (60 to 65°F), dark spot, like a basement or closet, and keep the medium damp by sprinkling it once a week or so. Cover the buckets with a paper or plastic bag to prevent light from reaching the roots. In about three to five weeks—depending on the temperature where you have stored them—tight-leaved pale yellow to white, cylindrical buds, known as "chicons," form above the root. Keeping them in the dark is impor-

tant because light turns them bitter.

When the chicons are four to five inches long, clip them from the root, clean them, and get ready to enjoy them. Eat them in salad, fill them with hummus or soft cheese for a healthy, crunchy alternative to crackers, braise them, steam them, or, like my grandmother did, bake them au gratin.

Keep the roots moist and in the dark, and they'll continue producing chicons until you're ready to start the outdoor growing season again.

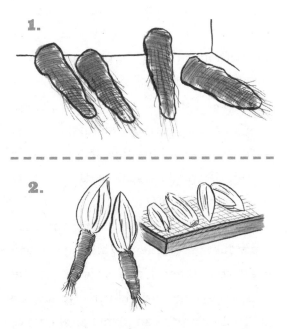

# Organic Answers

**Unless the food you buy in the grocery** store has a "USDA Certified Organic" label, it has been produced with a regime of herbicides, insecticides, fungicides, petroleum-based fertilizers, and postharvest treatments. Processed food that includes soy or corn as ingredients—check labels and you'll see nearly all have one or both of these—contain genetically modified organisms (known as GMOs), crops whose DNA has been altered to allow farmers to use more weed-killing chemicals without harming the plants.

This approach to producing food is best described, I think, as "industrial agriculture," although it is more commonly known as "conventional" (as opposed to organic) farming. Agricultural chemicals have been linked in the most credible scientific research to an increased risk of cancer and reproductive ailments among people exposed to them. There is also a growing body of evidence that industrial agriculture is causing significant damage to ecosystems near and far from the farms, such as the dramatic decline in honeybee populations documented in recent years and "dead zones" in the Gulf of Mexico. Many agricultural chemicals are made with petroleum. For my perspective, then, industrial agriculture is not healthy or sustainable, and needs to be replaced by methods that protect the well-being of farmers, the soil they depend on to grow their own crops each year, and all the living things that interact with the plants.

You may already know a lot about what's wrong with industrial agriculture, and that may be why you're interested in homesteading. I've raised these issues here not to frighten you about the food supply or to urge you to buy organic food (which I do strongly recommend), but rather to help you think about how you are caring for your own food garden, whether it's in the ground or containers, outside or in.

All of the information and advice I've given you so far meets the definition of "organic." I was the editor of the pioneering *Organic Gardening* magazine for seven years (and on the staff for more than twenty years), and I've seen in my own garden and countless others I've visited that organic methods work very well. If you're like most homesteaders today, you probably want to feed your family the freshest, healthiest food possible, and you care about the environment, too. So you start with the desire to garden organically.

The real test of your conviction begins when you are ready to fertilize your plants and again when bugs, weeds, and diseases show up. You may be tempted then by promises of miraculous growth for your plants and the annihilation of all problems with simple easy-to-apply formulas that are "degradable" or "harmless to the environment." I hope you'll take a moment to realize that no matter what the manufacturers say, garden chemicals at least undermine the purity of the food you're growing and at worst pose a health hazard to you, your family and pets, and every other living thing; plus, they are not necessary.

Does choosing to forgo the chemicals and use organic methods mean you have to settle for small yields from weak plants that are at the mercy of swarms of bugs? Definitely not. The strategies I'm sharing with you in this section have been tried and tested by farmers and gardeners for decades (centuries in some cases) and have proved effective over the long term. Organic methods not only match (and even surpass) the yields you get from using chemicals, they also cost you less. The organic approach depends mostly on stuff you find around your home, which surely will appeal to resourceful homesteaders. The organic approach, as you will see, is really just sensible gardening practices.

## RIGHT SITE

Plants growing in the conditions that suit them best are much less prone to stress and other problems and are better able to withstand and outgrow any problems that do arise. For most food crops, a very sunny location with loose fertile soil is ideal. If you try to grow food in a shady or soggy area, your yields will be lower and the plants are likely to be targeted by pests and diseases. All the miracle products available cannot help solve the problems of plants growing where they are not well-adapted. If you don't have a sunny, well-drained site to grow a garden, plant in containers and move them to where the sun is.

## FEED THE SOIL

Plants have evolved to extract the specific nutrients they need from the soil and take them up through their roots in the exact amounts they need. Further, plants have a symbiotic relationship with the billions of microbes in the soil that make nutrients available to them and protect their health. Fascinating recent research has even determined that plants' roots "farm" the particular microbes they need by sending out a hormonal signal. So, rather than force-feed premixed nutrients to your plants, you want to nurture the soil's microbe population. You do that by regularly adding organic matter, especially compost, to the soil. (Look for directions on how to make or get compost on page 178.) Mix compost into your garden soil or potting mix before planting. Every four to six weeks throughout the growing season, spread a half-inch layer of compost on top of the soil around your plants, scratch it in a little, and the microbes that live and feed on compost will nourish the plants for you.

## BUILT-IN RESISTANCE

Just as some people are inherently better able to ward off diseases than others, so are some plants. By observing which plants in each crop don't fall prey to viruses, wilts, and other ailments, breeders have been able to select for and develop hybrids with innate disease resistance. You can tell which have it when you buy seeds and plants because they are labeled with initials, such as TMV (tobacco mosaic virus) or F (fusarium wilt), representing the diseases they resist. If in previous seasons your area has been hit by plant diseases—you can confirm this with other local growers or your county's extension agent—resistant varieties are the best protection for you.

## DIG DIVERSITY

Farmers grow fields with row after row of the same crop because that organization lets them plant and harvest efficiently with machines. Trouble is, row layout also makes it easy for pests to find their favorite food and invite their cohorts for the feast. Your garden doesn't have to be laid out like a farm—and shouldn't be. When you plant, mix and match your vegetables and herbs in any pattern you like, or none at all. This keeps the bugs confused and slows the spread of plant diseases, many of which live in the soil and can be transmitted quickly from plant to plant.

## GRASPING THE FOOD CHAIN

The surest, safest way for you to protect your garden from pests is to take advantage of the food chain. Birds, toads, and snakes prey on bugs. Make your garden hospitable to them with shallow dishes of water for them to sip and places to perch or find shelter, and they'll hang around munching on pests. Plant flowers around your garden, especially tiny blossoms such as sweet alyssum or yarrow, to lure in the bugs that eat bugs that eat plants. Ladybug larvae, for instance, look like tiny orange alligators, and their favorite food is aphids, tiny flying insects that suck sap from plants. Ladybugs come for the nectar in the flowers and lay their eggs around your garden—when the larvae hatch, they dine on thousands of aphids. Many others of these "beneficial insects" are commonly attracted to gardens, from the familiar praying mantis and green lacewing to a wide array of different little wasps and flies that parasitize pests.

## OBSERVE, IDENTIFY, AND THEN REACT

So here's a not-very-bold prediction: Your garden will have bugs in it. Hundreds, even thousands of them. And I understand that when you see bugs, you may be distressed and wonder if all the work you've put into growing your food crop will be destroyed. But take a deep breath and watch. You'll see that most insects do not damage plants, and even when the buggers do chew leaves, the plants are often able to continue growing and producing anyway.

If you do notice pests infesting your crop, take note of exactly which plants they are damaging, where on the plant they are at work, and what type of damage they are doing. Most insects are specialists, so gathering this kind of information helps you to get a positive identification of it. When you are certain exactly what pest you are trying to control, you can pick a treatment that works against them. I'll tell you about a few simple, effective, and non-toxic options you can use.

## HAND OR HOSE

I always wait a couple days after I notice a pest infestation to do anything. First, I want to see if the plant is really suffering from the attack or continues to grow normally. Second, I want to give my natural allies—the birds, reptiles, and beneficial insects—a chance to resolve the problem before I act.

If the problem persists and I have to act, I try to think like a physician who assesses all the contributing factors and starts with the least invasive treatment. If the patient is suffering from stress—too little or too much water, for instance, or temperatures too high or too low—then no pest treatment will solve the problem. Pests are drawn to stressed-out plants, just as overly stressed people are more likely to get sick. You need to address the cause of the problem before you can solve the pest problem.

When a healthy plant is attacked, handpicking the bugs is a low-impact (and sometimes very gratifying) place to start. Drop the pests in a bucket or can filled with warm water and a tablespoon or so of liquid dishwashing soap. Don't like the idea of touching insects with your bare hands? I know a few gardeners who handpick bugs and slugs with chopsticks, which probably causes their neighbors to wonder just what they're doing with the bugs!

Tiny, flightless bugs like aphids can be squirted off plants with just a direct stream of water. They can't climb back up—they hatched on the plant from eggs laid by their winged parents, who don't eat plants. Check the undersides of leaves for egg clusters (usually a gelatinous or stringy mass), and squirt or scrape them off, too.

## ERECTING BARRIERS

You can keep pests off your plants in the first place with physical obstacles. Cutworms, for instance, can mow down a row of newly sprouted seedlings almost overnight. Make a little collar for each little plant out of cardboard or the order cards that fall out of magazines and catalogs, and the cutworms can't get to the stems. Row cover is a fabric made from very light fibers that let air, light, and water through but keep moths and other pests from landing on and laying eggs in your crops. (Reemay is the most widely known brand of row cover and is found in many nurseries and online.) Spread the row cover on top of the plants, and you keep the pests out. You may be able to substitute ordinary white cotton sheets, but the investment in the specially designed row cover is worth the expense, I think, because it works so well and you can use it season after season.

## HOUSEHOLD HELPERS

When all else fails and the time comes to hit the pests hard, you don't need to go nuclear and blast them with toxic chemicals. Two tablespoons of liquid dishwashing soap and a teaspoon of vegetable oil used for cooking mixed well into a quart of water makes a spray that washes a protective coating off soft-bodied insects such as thrips, which they cannot survive. Add a tablespoon of ordinary baking soda to the soap, oil, and water solution to make an antifungal spray for cucumbers, squash, and other plants.

To control slugs, a troublesome pest of lettuce, strawberries, and other crops growing in cool, damp conditions, sprinkle salt on their slimy backs and watch them shrivel up. Or set a plastic tub (like margarine comes in) in the soil so it is level with the ground and fill it up with beer (the dregs from your bottles work great), and check in the morning to see all the slugs attracted by the yeast who have drowned in it.

A spray made from pureed hot peppers and garlic with a teaspoon of oil in water drives off beetles, caterpillars, and other leaf-chewing pests.

Before using any homemade pest control spray on your plants, test it on a few leaves first to be sure it won't hurt the plant. Wait a few hours after the trial before you spray your whole crop. Remember to reapply sprays after a rainstorm.

Deer can also be deterred with a hot pepper spray—at least for a while. Other tactics that may keep deer at bay: bars of strong-smelling soap hung around the garden, the scent of a dog or even your scent (if you know what I mean—spread it discreetly) in the garden, lights, or sounds triggered by a motion detector, and whirligigs and anything else that moves unexpectedly. In some areas deer are so prevalent and accustomed to eating from home gardens that the only sure defense is a tall wire fence. Eight feet tall is ideal and, if possible, angled sway from the outside so that the deer may not be able to land clearly if they attempt to jump.

A fence that's just four feet high but that goes a couple feet underground keeps groundhogs (aka woodchucks), rabbits, and other critters out of your garden. Planting a trap crop is a less costly approach that often works for all of these pest animals. A trap crop is simply a bed full of inexpensive greens that you plant close to the edge of the woodland where the animals live. They get the food they're after in a place that feels safer to them and leave your garden alone.

Whichever pest-control strategies you choose, always keep in mind that you are not a farmer, and while you are growing food to provide for your family, your livelihood does not depend on the crop. So it is just not worth it to use dangerous chemicals to protect your garden. Better to let your garden be decimated—which it won't be if you consistently build your soil with compost and other organic matter.

# Saving Seeds

**A simple act of self-sufficiency,** practiced by farmers for generations, saving seeds from this season's crop to plant next year is worth more than just the money you save on buying seeds. You create strains of your favorite vegetable varieties that are uniquely adapted to your specific conditions. You might even help preserve biodiversity. Best of all, saving seeds requires no special equipment, and it's easy and fun.

I won't go too far into genetics or plant reproduction here, but I do need to explain a little to help you succeed with saving seeds. For most of the popular garden vegetables, you can find open-pollinated and hybrid varieties. "Open-pollinated" means that the seed comes from a plant that was pollinated from any other of its species nearby. Hybrids are created when plant breeders intentionally transfer the pollen of one plant to another with the goal of introducing desirable traits to them. (Please don't confuse this with genetic engineering, which involves the transfer of DNA in the laboratory from one organism to another. Hybridizing has been practiced for centuries and is known to be safe.) Seeds from open-pollinated varieties grow into plants with exactly the same attributes as the plants they came from. That's why you want to save open-pollinated seeds. You can save and replant the seeds from hybrids, but they may be sterile, and if not they are very likely to produce plants that are not just like their "parents." You can tell the difference when you're buying seeds to start with—look for "OP" or "F1 hybrid" on the seed packet or in the catalog description.

After you've planted your open-pollinated seeds and the plants begin to mature, take note about which have the traits you like most. Consider the flavor, texture, and color of the edible parts, as well as the plants' size, productivity, and resistance to problems. If you keep and replant the seeds from your best plants each year, you become like a plant breeder—selecting for the most desirable traits and encouraging them until your whole crop has those same attributes.

If other gardeners like those traits and want the strains you've created, you can swap your extras for other seeds you want. The Seed Savers Exchange (www.seed-savers.org) in Decorah, Iowa, was established in the 1970s to support and facilitate seed-swapping. You now can find many online forums where gardeners are swapping seeds, but through the Seed Savers Exchange you will be joining the community of gardeners and farmers who have kept alive some of the heirloom vegetables prized today. That's no exaggeration. The Brandywine tomato consistently wins taste tests every year. Thirty years ago it was no longer for sale from commercial seed companies, but seed savers kept growing and saving it; today you can easily buy it again. Industrial-scale farmers want tomatoes and other vegetables that are uniform in size and shape (so they can be easily picked by a machine) and able to withstand shipping to market. As a gardener, you can choose to grow varieties because they taste great, no matter what they look like. Saving seeds gives you access to the best varieties and keeps them available for others like you.

## EASIEST SEEDS FOR SAVING

If you look inside a packet of seeds for peas and beans, you'll notice that the seeds look a lot like peas and beans. So all you have to do to save seeds from those crops is to leave them on the vine until they are fully mature and have begun to dry. When the growing season is over, you then pluck the peas and beans from the their pods, put them in a paper bag in a cool, dry place, and leave them to continue drying for a couple weeks. When one of the seeds shatters from a hammer blow (indicating it's thoroughly dry), put the rest in a jar or envelope, mark it clearly with the variety and the year, and store them where you'll remember them next season. Many people use an old recipe card box for their saved seeds, which can help with organizing them when you have a lot. (When you've saved your seeds and are ready to plant, read the Appendix on page 221 for information on growing fruits, vegetables, and herbs of all kinds.)

## SEEDS VS. PLANTS

### BEST GROWN FROM SEEDS:

| | |
|---|---|
| Beans | Dill |
| Beets | Peas |
| Carrots | Radishes |
| Corn | Spinach |

### BEST GROWN FROM STARTED PLANTS:

| | |
|---|---|
| Basil | Peppers |
| Broccoli | Squash |
| Chives | Strawberries |
| Cucumbers | Tomatoes |
| Melons | |

### YOUR CHOICE:

Lettuce and other salad greens

Pepper seeds are clustered around the top, where the stem meets the flesh. When the pepper plant dies at the end of the season (this may not happen in warm climates), gather the pods you left to mature. Over a dish, rub the seeds loose with your finger and set them away from direct light for a week to dry. If you grew hot peppers, you probably have enough seeds to use some to make your own pizza seasoning (see page 97). Store the rest for replanting.

You might have noticed while you were planting that corn's kernels are its seeds. To get kernels ready for storage, leave the ears on the stalk until the husks turn brown and frost or diminishing daylight brings the plants' lives to a natural conclusion. Pull off the cobs, peel back the husk, and air-dry them until the kernels are hard, maybe three weeks or so. Scrape the seeds from the cob, then store them for the winter in jars or envelopes. One caution about saving corn seeds: they cross-pollinate so easily between varieties that if you grow more than one variety (or had a different one growing in sight of yours), the seeds will be hybrids by default and may yield unappealing results the following year. Experienced seed savers carefully separate different varieties of corn and other crops, like squashes, that are prone to cross-pollinating.

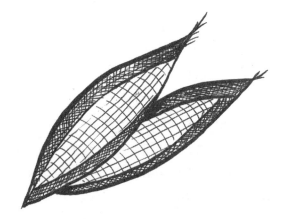

## SLOW SEEDS

Lettuce (and other salad greens) and dill produce their seeds long after you're finished eating them. Greens typically start to taste bitter and grow long, tough leaves as daylight hours increase and the temperature rises. A few weeks later a long stalk shoots up and tiny white or yellow flowers open up. Dill's top fronds form a spidery blossom with little yellowish flowers. After pollination the seeds are formed in the flowers. Cut the flowers when the plant dies—but don't wait too long; birds love these tiny seeds—and put them in paper bags to dry for a couple weeks. Holding each flower over a dish, rub with your hands to loosen the seeds. If they're not all fully dry, let them sit in the open air for a day or two before you store them.

## MESSY SEEDS

The seeds in tomatoes, cucumbers, and squash are wet when you harvest them, so you need to treat them differently. Let a few of the fruits mature to the point where they are about to—or maybe already have—fallen off the vines. Lightly mash the fruit open, then put it in a bucket with a few cups of warm water (enough to cover the pulp and then one more). For the next three or four days, stir the mixture each day. You'll see mold growing on top. Seeds that won't grow float in the mold, while the viable seeds sink to the bottom. When you see that happen, pour off the mold (yuck, I know), gather the good seeds, and rinse them off. Leave them to dry for a few days on paper plates, and they're ready for you to store them.

If you can, you want to plant all the seeds you saved the following season, or trade all of your extras, because seeds' germination rates decline—to varying degrees—in storage. But if you do happen to forget some, test them before you toss them. Here's how you can test seeds' viability: Put a few in a damp paper towel, roll them up inside of a resealable plastic bag, and keep them moist for a week in the refrigerator. If they've sprouted in a week, they're still ready for planting.

## WELL-AGED SEEDS

*Though seeds don't come with an exact expiration date,* they do lose their viability over time. With each season, fewer of them will germinate. But before you toss away old seeds, consider this: In 2005 scientists planted a date palm seed discovered in excavations at Herod the Great's palace in Israel. The seed, estimated using carbon-dating to be 2,000 years old, germinated and produced a tree. I once spoke to a gardener who found a stash of tomato seeds that had been in his grandfather's barn for 80 years. The gardener planted the seed and 80% of them sprouted and grew into healthy, vigorous tomato plants. Now those were some true heirloom tomatoes!

# CHAPTER TWO

# GOING WILD FOR FOOD

**F**oraging for food is for contestants on reality shows and desperate people who are really lost in the wilderness, right? Well, if you are a modern home-steader looking for ways to add more fresh, locally sourced food to your diet, you can find a wide variety of vegetables, fruits, nuts, and fungi with unique, delicious fla-vors just waiting for you to gather them up. In many instances, foraged foods are even more nutritious than the cultivated and processed items you buy at the store. But all that aside, gathering food from the wild is a fun way to see how almost miraculously Nature works, even in places where it appears to be overwhelmed by manmade habitat.

You don't have to live near the prairie or the forest to be close to edible wild food. You'll find it around old houses, in vacant city lots, even in your own backyard. In fact, I'll bet there's something uncultivated that you can eat within a five-minute walk from your front door—you just never noticed.

# FORAGE WITH CAUTION

BEFORE WE GET INTO THE SPECIFICS, I HAVE TO GIVE YOU A FEW CRITICAL words of caution. Most important: Before you eat any wild food, be sure you have absolutely, positively identified it. Many common edible wild foods have poisonous (or at least unpalatable) look-alikes. Check a credible guidebook (see the "Resources" section on page 000 for suggestions), or ask an experienced forager to confirm your identification. Don't trust common name identification; rather, rely on the scientific names. Very different plants can be known by the same colloquial name, but each plant and fungus has its own unique genus and species designation.

Also, don't eat anything that could possibly have been treated with insecticides, herbicides, or fungicides. Wild plants are not normally treated with these chemicals, but if they come from an area with cultivated plants, they may have been sprayed as part of a treatment program for a lawn or other domestic space. If you have doubts about whether a plant has been sprayed or not, pass on eating it.

So with those cautions in mind, you are ready to step outside and into the world of wild food. I believe you'll be surprised by all the options you have and how accessible they are to you, wherever you live.

# Vegetables

**The greens that we eat every day—** or at least should eat every day—are in many cases simply cultivated cousins of wild plants that grow by themselves. Many of them come up in early spring, though some thrive in the hot temperatures of summer when the lettuce, spinach, and other salad greens in your garden wilt or go to seed. In nearly every case, the newest, smallest leaves are the tenderest and the best-tasting. (This is actually true of most cultivated vegetables, too—as they get larger, they become chewier, drier, or pulpier and develop bitter or harsh flavors. "Pick young and often" is a good rule of thumb for most food plants.) The list of wild vegetables you can eat is very long; here I will introduce you to those most frequently found in cities and suburbs.

*dandelions*

*Dandelions.* The most common lawn weed, the scourge of suburbanites who meticulously tend their swaths of turf, is a tasty salad ingredient that is gathered each spring by cooks in France, Italy, and other areas around the Mediterranean. If you don't find dandelions near you but still want some, you can come by and pick them out of my lawn. Seriously, you can buy seeds to plant from suppliers that specialize in Italian varieties or unusual greens. Dandelions come up as the days begin to warm in early spring, so you can harvest them before the first greens of the season are ready to be harvested from your garden. When the leaves are small, they look and taste very much like arugula, but cost a lot less than the $2.99 or more per pound that you pay for gourmet greens in the supermarket. Like arugula, they have a lightly bitter flavor that becomes more pronounced as the days grow warmer. Dandelions are best eaten fresh and raw, blended with other sweeter greens such as Bibb lettuce. You can also braise them with garlic in olive oil as you would spinach or kale. The flowers and stems are the raw ingredients for dandelion wine.

*Corn salad*

**Corn salad.** Another early spring weed you can eat, corn salad is also known as lamb's lettuce or, to the hippest foodies, mâche. It grows in a little rosette, or head, and its spoon-shaped leaves are mild, even sweet, and they have more iron than spinach. Corn salad is also a good vegetable source of omega-3 fatty acids. It can be found in some areas in autumn as well as spring. Seed companies offer mâche, if you can't find it and want to grow your own. Harvest just the leaves when they are three to four inches tall, or pull the whole plant and then cut off the root. Either way, pick it before it starts to flower as the days get warmer. Leave a few to flower and produce seed, and you'll have more to enjoy next season.

*Lamb's Quarters*

**Lamb's quarters.** You may not know it by name, but if you've tended a garden or lawn, you've seen lamb's quarters. It is also known as white goosefoot (or just goosefoot) or pigweed. In India the plant is cultivated and eaten like spinach. You can harvest the leaves and the very tender young shoots that come up in early spring, and steam or braise them like you do with other greens. Just be aware that it is even higher in oxalic acid than spinach, which for some people disrupts their absorption of calcium. After lamb's quarters flowers, it also produces thousands of tiny, protein-rich seeds you can dry and eat. (A close relative, quinoa, is grown for its seeds, which are eaten as a grain.)

*Mustard*

**Mustard.** A member of the brassica family, which includes broccoli, cabbage, and radishes, mustard greens are the tough kinds of plants that flourish in abandoned lots, along railroad tracks, and other places where people once disturbed the natural plants but are now neglected.

Wild mustard comes up in early spring and flowers as soon as the days start getting long. The leaves have a peppery flavor that spices up braised greens and stir-fries. The seeds come after the flowers. You can grind them up and mix them with vinegar to make your own mustard for hot dogs and sandwiches.

*Chickweed*

**Chickweed.** Where grass is sparse in lawns and in bare spots in gardens, chickweed moves in during spring, fall, and even winter in many areas, growing close to the ground in an ever-expanding mat of thin stems and small leaves. This is a very common plant, but be absolutely sure to get a positive identification on it.

Poisonous spotted spurge and inedible knotweed also grow close to the ground and look similar to chickweed.

Chickens do love chickweed and it's nutritious for them, so you can gather it for your hens even if you don't want to eat it yourself. The stems and the leaves are both edible. Raw, they taste a bit like corn silk—fine if it comes along with the juicy sweet flavor of fresh corn, but maybe not enticing otherwise. Cooked chickweed will remind you of spinach, but with a little hint of lemon. Steam or braise it for no longer than five minutes, or you'll have nothing left to eat of the slim stems and leaves.

*Salad burnet*

**Salad burnet.** An herb cultivated in countries around the Mediterranean and Asia, salad burnet is a tall, very drought-tolerant perennial plant found in sunny open spaces like meadows and grassy fields. It survives year-round in much of North America, but it's at its best early in spring when the leaves are small and tender. Crush those leaves and you get a strong scent of cucumbers. You can eat the leaves raw in salads or use them as an herb to flavor dressings and dips. Salad burnet is a trendy cocktail ingredient in the hippest bars.

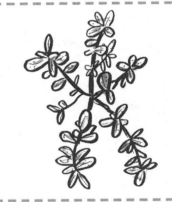

*Purslane*

**Purslane.** When summer heats up, purslane shows up in gardens, pathways, even sidewalk cracks. It is a succulent, which means its thick red stems and rounded, fleshy leaves retain water. Those stems and leaves have a tangy flavor and they hold up well to cooking in omelets and quiches, or sautéed with a bit of oil, lemon juice, and fresh herbs. In Mexico, purslane is known as *verdolagas*, and the leaves are boiled and served in a warm tortilla. You also can eat it raw in a salad or pickle the stems.

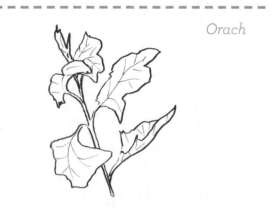

*Orach*

**Orach.** Also known as saltbush, orach looks like a taller type of lamb's quarters. It grows up to three feet tall in sandy, salty soil, which is why you'll find it near beaches, marshes, and other coastal areas. In late spring and early summer, pick the young leaves—they can reach up to five inches long, but you want them half that size. Their naturally salty flavor makes them a good companion with other greens in salads and cooked dishes.

*Wild garlic and onions.* Look at lawns after the first few warm days in spring, before the grass starts growing, and you'll see the tall, thin leaves of wild garlic and onions. The most immediately noticeable difference between them: Wild garlic has round, hollow leaves; wild onion leaves are flat. But they differ very little from the chives and scallions you buy in the grocery store. You can just use the leaves to add flavor to soups and stews, or dig up the bulbs to cook as you would shallots.

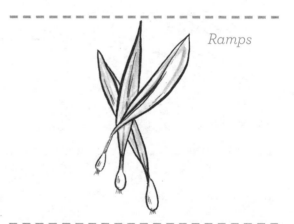

*Ramps*

**Ramps.** Another wild member of the onion family, ramps (or wild leeks) have wider leaves and small, spicy bulbs. They grow in damp, sandy soil, frequently near streams and creeks. They come up in late winter and early spring—when towns in West Virginia and other states hold festivals to celebrate the crop—and typically last for just a few weeks. When ramps first come up is the best time to eat the small tender leaves, chopped and added to any dish that calls for chives. You can eat the bulbs into early summer, when heat turns them bitter. Add them to fried potatoes, sauté them with bacon, pickle, or grill them.

keep them whiter in color and more tender. Cardoon soup is a traditional start to Easter dinner in some regions of Italy. It's also an ingredient in *Cocido madrileno*, a one-pot meal that's one of Spain's national dishes. Cardoon stems—you can eat the flower buds, but there isn't much to them—taste similar to artichokes and can be steamed, braised, cooked into broth, or battered and fried.

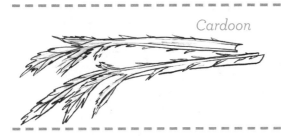

*Cardoon*

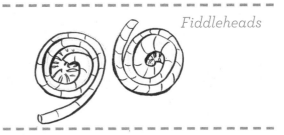

*Fiddleheads*

**Cardoon.** Artichokes are a cultivated cousin to the tall prickly thistle that is a pest to farmers and gardeners nearly everywhere in North America. Another relative, cardoon is gathered for its stems (the part of the artichoke we eat are the flowers) in late spring and early summer. Many who collect cardoon (or, as it's known among Italians, *cardoni*) find it growing in early spring and mound soil around the stems to

*Fiddleheads.* In early spring, ostrich ferns poke new shoots up through the ground that are coiled and wrapped in a papery sheath. When the shoots, or fiddleheads, are a couple inches tall, you can cut them off, peel away the wrapper, rinse them clean, and enjoy their unique mushroomy but still vegetal flavor. You can sauté them with onions and garlic and serve over pasta or in an omelet, or steam them for about 20 minutes, then top with melted butter. They're also great in a creamy soup or risotto.

## Wild Fruit

**Picking wild berries sounds like** something from a novel set in nineteenth-century America, doesn't it? But even while development has "paved paradise and put up a parking lot," berry bushes still hold on in the nooks and crannies of empty lots, playgrounds, backyards, and many other places where you may not have noticed them. (You can thank a bird for spreading the seeds wherever they land. Think about that next time you curse because your car is splattered with purple bird droppings.) Wild and just uncared-for fruit trees are ripe for picking in many cities and towns, where they were planted years ago and have long since been forgotten or ignored. If you look beyond the surface in most developed areas, at the edges of parking lots, housing subdivi-

sions, and highways, you'll find a surprising variety of fresh, local fruit, free for the picking. But I can't say this enough: Be absolutely sure you know what you are picking. Always try a small amount of any foraged food and wait to see if you have a reaction to consuming it before you eat a basket full of it.

*Raspberries, black raspberries, and blackberries.* These brambles—the group of berries that grow on long, arching canes with thorns—can certainly be planted and cultivated in your backyard. As satisfying as that is, it's no match for the simple joy of discovering a patch and filling a pail with wild berries. All three of these are found in damp, partially shaded environments. Black raspberries (which can cost $5 or more a pint at the grocery store or farmer's market) are actually the most common, but also the smallest and most fragile. You are more likely to find blackberries in a state park than in town. They can grow canes up to six feet tall, and the berries are typically as big as your thumb. When fully ripe and at their peak of sweetness, all of these berries just fall off the cane and drop into your palm when you tickle them a little with your fingers.

*Wineberries*

*Wineberries.* At first glance, you might think wineberries are raspberries. The plants and the fruit look very similar. But raspberries are deep red when they're at their ripest; wineberries are more fire-truck red. I see wineberries growing every summer in the wooded edge of my backyard, and also around the retention basin where I walk the dog, in the strip of land between two housing developments, and in the unmowed area behind the strip mall. Wineberry is considered, in many states, an "invasive" plant, which means that it adapts so well to most conditions that it

becomes a bully that outcompetes native species, threatening biodiversity. All of which means that you shouldn't plant them, but there's no reason not to gather and eat them where they are already growing. They're a little blander and a little more tart than raspberries—they're better combined with other fruits in pies and jams than eaten all alone.

*Salmonberries*

*Salmonberries, thimbleberries, and cloudberries.* In the Pacific Northwest, Alaska, and Canada, you can gather a few rare, tasty relatives of raspberries. They're all most commonly found in undeveloped areas, like the many national parks and other protected lands in the region. Salmonberries are pale yellow to deep orange when they're ripe, and they grow on canes up to six feet tall. Thimbleberries

*Thimbleberries*

look like small raspberries, though they're a little brighter red, but you can recognize them because the canes don't have thorns. Cloudberries, which look like golden blackberries, grow closer to the ground. They're all varying degrees of sweet, with a hint of tartness, and all very fragile when ripe, which is why they are not valued for commercial production but perfect for enterprising foragers.

*Cloudberries*

*Blueberries and huckleberries.* If you happen to find blueberries growing untended in a city or town, they were almost certainly planted by someone who since left them behind. The best places to look for them are around old homes, nurseries, and other abandoned buildings, especially in low-lying damp areas. Because blueberries and huckleberries look so much alike, people sometimes use the names interchangeably, though they are two distinct plants. They can both be colored from dusky blue to nearly black, and they ripen in late summer. The most noticeable difference between them is the seeds. Blueberries have many, but they're small; huckleberries have ten or fewer, but they're larger and crunchier. Both of them make delicious pie filling or jam, or add a sweet and juicy accent to pancakes and muffins.

One heads-up to remember when picking wild blueberries and huckleberries in a forest: they are a favorite food of bears. Be alert, especially early in the morning and in the late afternoon, for the sounds and signs of bears in the area, and back off the berries if you see or hear them.

*Mulberries*

*Elderberries*

*Mulberries.* Native to China, white mulberry trees were introduced to North America in the colonial days to nurture silkworms. Red mulberries were already growing in the wild. Today, you'll find both of them—along with another non-native to this continent, black mulberries—growing in city parks, in suburban yards, and along streets in nearly every climate. The berries hang in clusters from the tree and ripen in late spring and early summer. They're sweet with a slight hint of acid and are very high in a few unique antioxidant nutrients. If you find more than you can eat right away, mulberries, like other berries, dry very readily into tasty little pellets of flavor you can add to granola or trail mix. Mulberry wine might not replace your favorite merlot, but it has its fans.

*Elderberries.* A North American native—though they're found on nearly every other continent, too—elderberries grow on shrubs that can reach thirteen feet tall. They favor moist conditions and in developed areas show up in the thickets around streambeds and retention basins. Their lacy, white flowers open in late spring to early summer. The flowers make a light, fragrant tea, are used to make syrup or liqueur, and often are included in herbal remedies. There's even a soft drink popular in Europe made from elder flowers, called Fanta Shokata. The dark blue-almost black berries ripen from midsummer to fall. The easiest way to harvest them is to pick the whole clusters (rather than berry by berry), place them in the freezer when you get home, and an hour later the berries will fall right off the branch. They taste bitter when eaten raw, but drying them seems to moderate that. Cooking brings out the best flavor, which is why elderberries make such popular jelly and pie filling. They're most in demand, though, for making wine or brandy. By the way, *Sambucus* is the plant's genus name, but the Italian liqueur called Sambuca is flavored with star anise, not elderberry.

In some regions you might find red elderberries. They are quite bitter and may be toxic to you, so pass on them. Also, elderberry bushes have no thorns. The shrub and fruit of Hercules Club look similar to elderberries, but the branches have short spines and the berries are poisonous. Check for thorns before you pick elderberries.

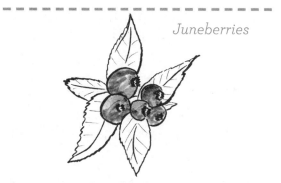

*Juneberries*

*Juneberries.* Shadbush, also known as Juneberry, is a very adaptable shrub that grows in a wide variety of conditions throughout North America. Birds flock to the fruit and then spread the seeds far and wide to almost any untended area you find, and the shrubs are so attractive year-round and maintenance-free that many landscapers today use them in their plantings around office parks, condominium complexes, and housing developments. The different common names by which these shrubs are known tell you about their timing. They bloom with clusters of white flowers in early spring—before nearly every other tree and shrub—at about the same time shad begin their annual spawning run up rivers and streams in the Northeast. The berries ripen in June. When fully ripe, they look a lot like blueberries. But they taste more like pears, which seems weird until you know that the plant is in the apple family. You can eat the berries fresh right off the branch or use them in muffins or cobblers. Like apples, the berries are naturally high in pectin, so they cook readily into a thick pie filling.

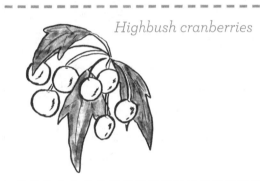

*Highbush cranberries*

**Highbush cranberries.** Not actually related to the cranberries we eat on Thanksgiving (which are in the same family as blueberries), highbush cranberries have also become a popular ornamental plant for city parks and corporate campuses. They don't need a bog, but they do grow best in partly shady, moist areas. The shrubs get to be about four feet tall, bloom with little white flowers in late spring, and bear little red berries that look just like Thanksgiving cranberries in late summer. And they have a slightly sour taste, which some say sweetens if you pick them after the frost. Of course, by then it's likely birds will have eaten them. You won't want to eat a lot of them fresh off the shrub—besides the sour taste, they have a large seed inside. But you can use them in any recipe that calls for cranberries, like sauces and stuffing.

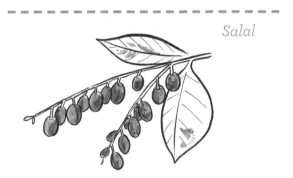

*Salal*

**Salal.** The name sounds more like a dish on the menu at a Middle Eastern restaurant than a shrub native to the western United States. But salal is a relative of azaleas and rhododendrons most often found growing in woodlands and other untended areas. Its leathery leaves are commonly used to give heft to flower arrangements. Salal berries are the same color as blueberries, but they are oblong rather than round and seedy. They ripen in midsummer. Their flavor is lightly tart and blends well with grapes in preserves and other berries in pies and cobblers.

*Gooseberries and currants.* Just a couple generations back these closely related plants were a fixture in every backyard. But while few people plant them (or any other fruit) in their yards anymore, gooseberries and currants have long since escaped cultivation and now grow wild just about everywhere in North America, including coastal areas. Look for them around old homes and fields. You won't find it easy to tell gooseberries and currants from each other—there are many diverse varieties of each—but they both bear lots of small, grapelike fruit on shrubs that are two to five feet tall. The fruit have a pleasant tart flavor when they're green—in mid- to late summer. Many people use the green berries for jelly (they're naturally high in pectin). In early fall they ripen to deep red and become sweeter, and excellent for pies. In places where winter is mild, the fruit that remains on the shrub will turn into sun-dried raisins.

*Grapes.* I'm willing to bet you won't have to look far from your home to find wild grapes, no matter where you live. With the dozens of different varieties that have evolved, grapes are found growing wild in nearly every climate. Among the many varieties, fox grapes and muscadine grapes are considered the best tasting. In coastal areas, sea grapes (a different plant family from true grapes) thrive in sandy soil and windy conditions. I've seen grapevines climbing the concrete wall of a semidemolished building, on poles at railroad sidings, and in a stand of the only three tall trees left near a playground. The fruit is more like Concord grapes than the "table grapes" you get at the supermarket. That is, they are dark blue or purple when fully ripe, they have a few seeds inside, and the flavor is a balance of tart and sweet. They ripen from late summer to early fall. You can use wild grapes in all the same ways as domesticated ones: for jelly, juice and wine, or eating fresh—if you don't mind spitting seeds.

*Crabapples.* Dazzling, ruffly pink flowers that open at the height of spring have made crabapples a favorite small tree of many landscapers. Remember where you see them in bloom—around office buildings, malls, and homes—and come back in late summer to gather the tart little fruits when they're ruby red. They're tart when raw, but cooking changes their flavor to acidy sweet. Pickled with spices like cloves and cinnamon, they make a classic condiment to serve alongside cranberry sauce and whole grain mustard. Crabapples are the easiest member of the large apple family to find in the wild, but it's not the only one that you might run across growing untended. If you live close to land that used to be a farm, chances are the remnants of an apple orchard are somewhere nearby. The fruit won't look like the polished brilliance of the giant Red Delicious stacked up in the supermarket—it's more likely to be varying shades of red and green, perhaps with dry brown russet patches—but they'll taste like a summer full of sunshine and rainstorms.

*Plums.* If you know plums as baseball-sized, dark purple skinned fruit with yellow or red flesh—that is, the fruit sold in supermarkets in summer—you might not recognize the dozens of other varieties that grow in just about every region of North America. Wild plums tend to be smaller—some closer to the size of a large cherry or grape—and come in a wide range of skin colors, including cherry red, pale green, and sunny yellow. When fully ripe (in mid- to late summer), they are sweet, but with the hint of must like you taste when you bite into wild grapes. Many plum trees were planted for their ornamental qualities—the trees top out at about 25 feet tall, and they bloom in a flurry of white petals in spring around homes and along streets in town centers in the East and Midwest. Chances are, you've passed by untended plums in your area and just never noticed. One very common variety, the sand plum, grows wild in the southern United States from Texas and Oklahoma east. As you might guess from the name, they favor sandy soil and tend to grow into thickets in coastal areas. You can make any wild plums into a sweet and potent liqueur by soaking them in vodka, or you can use them to make wine, jelly, or pie.

*Maypop*

**Maypop.** Tropical passion fruit has a cold-hardy cousin that thrives along the edges of fields, roadside ditches, and other open sunny areas in the southern United States. In early spring it sports bright purple flowers on vines wrapped around shrubs and small trees. By early summer the vines are hung with rather large (almost the size of an average chicken

egg) green berries that turn to yellow and, when dead-ripe, drop off the vine. They're popular with all kinds of wildlife, so you'll have to be timely if you want to gather them. Maypops taste like other passion fruit—hints of melon, pineapple, guava—though they are very seedy. Some people go to the trouble of deseeding maypop, but the seeds are not harmful for you to eat. Just pop them in your mouth fresh, add them to a smoothie, or reduce them to a sweet syrup.

*Hawthorn*

**Haws.** The hawthorn is a small tree with prickly spines on the branches. Those spines made it a popular choice for hedgerows planted to keep wildlife out of or livestock inside a property. Now you'll see hawthorns in thickets and other untamed areas, especially where old homesteads used to be. The fruit, called haws, are about the size and shape of an olive, ripen to dark red, are pulpy, and have one to five seeds. The haws are bitter when young, but after a few hard frosts, they sweeten into an applelike flavor. You can use them in mixed fruit preserves and sauces for meats.

*Pawpaw*

**Pawpaw.** In woodlands throughout most of North America, pawpaw trees bear the largest edible fruit native to this continent. Pawpaws can weigh up to a pound each and look similar to mangoes. When ripe, the fruit is soft and thin-skinned, maturing from green to yellow as they ripen. The flavor calls to mind bananas and mangoes. You almost have to eat them fresh off the trees, as they are so fragile they are hard to keep for any length of time.

**Persimmons.** You may know Japanese (or Asian) persimmons as a specialty fruit found in grocery stores only during certain times of the year. They are tennis-ball size, bright orange, and, until soft and ripe, very astringent. The native American persimmon grows wild throughout the East and South, in semi-open areas where the medium-size trees can get sun. The fruit is smaller than the Asian type—an inch or so in diameter, on average. American persimmons are also very sour before they ripen (typically after the first frost), but when they reach that point where they are falling off the tree, they are as sweet as any fruit you'll eat this side of grapes. If you want to gather some before the squirrels, chipmunks, and other wildlife take them all, you can harvest them before they fall off the tree and let them finish softening in your fruit bowl inside. You can eat American persimmons raw or make them into a traditional pudding.

*Chokecherries*

*Chokecherries.* For the Native Americans who lived on the northern Plains, chokecherries were an important staple food that was very abundant and easy to gather. Today, they thrive where people have disturbed the land. Look for them around neglected fields and fencerows, along roadsides and clearings, culverts and wetlands. Chokecherries, which are in the same family as domesticated cherries, plums, and peaches, grow on thin-stemmed shrubs that reach up to twenty feet tall. The fruit looks very similar to black cherries you buy in the store, but chokecherries can be quite astringent, especially when they're picked too soon. You want to leave them on the bush until they lose their red color and have all turned dark purple, almost black. They

typically start to ripen around the middle of August and continue into early September. Don't rush this. When you are picking them, keep an eye out for stinkbugs, which frequent chokecherry bushes—you don't want to let one of them sneak into your bucket and inadvertently bite into one of them. The ripe fruit makes delicious jelly and a thick, sweet syrup you can pour on pancakes or desserts. Or preserve them as the natives did—dried to a sweet chewiness—and then add them to your cereal, muffin batter, or granola.

*Prickly Pear*

*Prickly pear.* A wide variety of cactus species flourish in the deserts in the Southwest, but one cactus grows wild in dry areas throughout the United States. Though there are several species, they are all low-growing and have familiar-looking fleshy pads and sharp spines. They flower at different times of the season, depending on the species and climate, with bright yellow, red, or purple flowers, which turn into bumpy grape-size fruit that ripens to dark pink or red. They have clusters of tiny barbed spines on their outer skin, so you need to handle them with gloves and slice open and peel away the skin before you eat the fruit. Prickly pears, sometimes sold in stores as "tuna" (as they're known in Mexico), are full of juice that reminds some people of sugar-free bubblegum and others of watermelon. You can use it to flavor candy, sauces, salad dressing, cake frosting, or cocktails. Many people, especially of Mexican heritage, also eat the pads as a fried or steamed vegetable, called *nopalitos*.

# Nuts

**Every autumn, trees of many differ**ent types drop pounds and pounds of healthy, protein-rich food at your feet. Acorns, chestnuts, black walnuts, and other kinds of nuts fall from trees onto streets, sidewalks, and walking paths, and any that are not quickly gathered up by squirrels and chipmunks are likely to be swept up and into the trash. You can beat them to it and take home a supply of fresh food you can snack on or use to make meals and desserts.

*Acorns.* You don't have to be a squirrel to appreciate acorns. They are, like other nuts, high in protein, but they're lower in fat than many others. And you won't have to look far for them. Oak trees are everywhere in North America—city parks and country fields, backyards and forests. In a single fall season, a small oak tree can drop twenty-five pounds or more of acorns; big old oaks produce as much as a thousand pounds of them. You want to look for white (rather than red) varieties of oak. Bitter-tasting tannins are in every acorn, but those from white oaks tend to have the least. You can pick up acorns that have already fallen, or you can bring the acorns to you by spreading a tarp or sheet under the tree and shaking the limbs until the nuts fall. When you've gathered up your haul, crack the shells and pile up all the kernels that are yellowish (not black and dusty, a sign of insect damage). Native Americans set baskets of shelled acorns in clean fast-flowing streams, which would leach out the tannins in a couple of days. If you don't have a stream handy or want to speed up the process, boil the kernels for about fifteen minutes, dump the brown tannic water, and boil them again in fresh water. Keep up the boiling and dumping until the water no longer turns brown. (And if you have trouble removing the kernels from their shells, you can leave the acorns in their shells the first time you boil them.) After you've boiled away the tannins, you can roast the acorns in your oven at its lowest setting (about 175°F) for twenty minutes to make them crunchy and ready to eat like you would any other nut. Or you can use a mortar and pestle or hand-powered food mill to turn them into meal or flour for baking bread or pancakes.

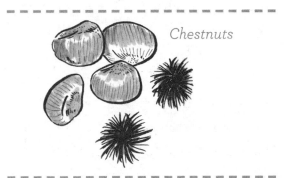

*Chestnuts*

**Chestnuts.** American chestnut trees used to be almost as abundant as oaks—that's a pretty big *almost*, but four billion (no exaggeration) American chestnut trees in forests and around old homes died in the early 1900s from chestnut blight, a disease accidentally imported from Asia. Today there are a few isolated stands of American chestnut trees left while research and breeding efforts continue to try to reestablish them. In the meantime, blight-resistant Chinese chestnut trees have been planted in their place and are thriving along streets, and in parks and woodlands. Like acorns, chestnuts drop from trees in the fall and are easy to gather, if you beat the squirrels and other wildlife to them. Chestnuts are also high in bitter tannins—not as much as acorns, but still too much for most people's taste. Prepare to remove the chestnuts' shells by slicing an "X" into the flat side. After you boil or roast them for about fifteen minutes to quell the tannic acid, peel back the shell while the chestnuts are still warm. (There's no need for the repeat boiling with chestnuts.) Want to roast them over an open fire, as the familiar Christmas song rhapsodizes? Puncture the nuts' shells to release steam as they cook, and put them in a metal basket or grate over white-hot coals. (You can also buy a chestnut roaster for your fireplace.)

You can eat chestnuts fresh roasted or add them to a traditional stuffing recipe. You can puree boiled or cooked kernels and use them in cooked dishes in place of potatoes or pasta—chestnuts are very high in starch—or as a thickener in soup and stew. In many countries, chestnuts are a popular ingredient in desserts. For instance, the classic Italian cake, Monte-bianco, is made with pureed chestnuts and whipped cream.

*Black Walnuts*

**Black walnuts.** You could pay $10 per pound or more for the most prized of walnuts, or you could be lucky enough to know where a black walnut tree is growing untended, near a neglected field or homestead. If you do, most likely it was planted generations back because its wood was highly valued for its beauty and strength. In early fall, when the black walnut tree's leaves turn golden yellow, so do the husks of the tennis-ball-size nuts. If you press on the spongy husk with your thumb and it makes an indentation, the nuts are ripe. At that stage, though, most of them are still on the tree, where squirrels have an easier time getting to them than you do. If you can, get at them with a ladder. If not, you'll have wait until after a frost or two for them to drop to the ground. Check often and pick them up as soon as possible to prevent them from rotting or becoming infested with worms.

Husking black walnuts is a messy job—wear old clothes and gardening gloves because the husks leave behind very stubborn brown stains on anything they touch. You can smash the husks open with a hammer or stomp them with your feet. Rinse the shelled nuts you find inside—but don't soak them—then spread them out on an old window screen or tray in a cool, well-ventilated place where rodents won't get to them and let them dry for a couple weeks. Crack open one of the shells, and check to see that the kernel inside snaps crisply. When it does, the walnuts are ready for storage in a cloth bag or a basket (protected from critters) in a well-ventilated place. Get them out when you're ready to make chocolate chip cookies, cakes, breads—or eat right out of your hand.

## MAST YEAR

THOUGH TREES LOOK TO BE STANDING still, minding their own business, they are engaged in complex and mysterious communication with the rest of their ecosystem. Oaks, chestnuts, pine, spruce, and other nut-bearing trees produce an extra-heavy crop one year, and then for the next few years yield a smaller amount. And they do it in sync with one another (all the oaks have a big year together) in an unpredictable pattern.

Scientists have tested lots of theories about the cause for a season of extra abundance, known as a "mast year." Weather, predator populations, and survival strategy all have been explored and may be factors, but as of yet nobody has proposed a complete, irrefutable explanation.

Understanding the mast year cycle is important to you as a forager. You want to be aware of when the ground is deep in chestnuts, acorns, or other nuts so that you can collect as much as possible when they are abundant and then be prepared for a smaller harvest for the next couple seasons.

**Caution:** Don't put the black walnut husks in your compost pile. All parts of this tree contain juglone, a naturally occurring compound that can keep garden plants from growing properly. If you have the space to plant your own black walnut, be sure to site it far from your garden.

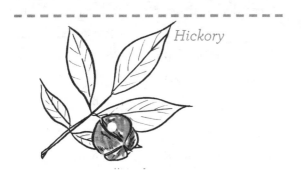

*Hickory*

*Hickory and other nuts.* Just as you can find untended fruit trees in overlooked places in cities and towns, you may also come across hickory trees and even domesticated nuts like hazelnuts and pecans planted where they've been long forgotten. You are most likely to find hickories. The nuts taste similar to pecans and are harvested, husked, cured, and stored just as you would black walnuts.

# Fun with Fungi

**I've already given you at the start of** this chapter the critical warnings about collecting wild foods cautiously, taking care to positively identify your harvest before you eat it. I'm bringing up the warnings again before we delve into mushroom-hunting because it is so important that you heed them. Mushrooms are not more toxic than plants, and the woods are not full of lethal fungi looking as innocent as a pizza topping. The fact is, only a dozen or fewer of the mushrooms found in North America will cause you serious harm (such as death or illness). And with a little experience and a trustworthy guidebook, you'll have no trouble recognizing them. But the vast majority of mushrooms found in the wild don't taste good. So you want to focus your time and energy only on the good ones.

Go first with an experienced mushroom hunter, if you can find one. Many metropolitan areas have mushroom-hunting clubs whose members can be a great source of information and guidance. Before you go alone, if you must, take the time to learn what the most prevalent edible mushrooms look like and where they're found. You don't want to waste your time and effort gathering up every fungi you see.

The best place to look for mushrooms varies depending on the type, but the most likely locations for many kinds are around fallen logs and dead standing trees and in the leaf litter found at the base of living trees. When you find one, cut the whole fruit (yes, scientifically speaking, it is a fruit of the underground fungus), including both cap and stem. If you find mushrooms that look weathered or withered, pass on them. Put the clean, healthy-looking mushrooms in paper or wax bags—not plastic, which traps humidity that spoils their flavor and texture. Make a note on the bag or on a piece of paper about exactly where you found them. This isn't just bookkeeping: when you look at your guidebook, it will tell you where and how the mushrooms you're trying to identify grow. You want to be sure you have an exact match between the guidebook description and your notes, and whether you found the mushroom on a fallen log or standing tree makes a difference.

You can find a wide variety of mushrooms to pick, many unique to the region where you live. I'll get you started by telling you a bit about five of the most common.

*Morels*

**Morels.** Among the most popular wild mushrooms, morels pop up in groups from spring to early summer in the litter beneath hardwood trees. The brown caps are patterned with clearly defined pits and ridges, and the bottom edge of the cap is always attached directly to the stem. They can be as large as a foot tall, though ones shorter than six inches are tenderer than the big ones. Enjoy them sautéed briefly in butter. If you're lucky enough to find more than you can eat right away, they dry and keep very well (see page 92 for more about drying).

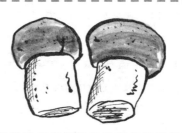

*Boletes*

*Chanterelles*

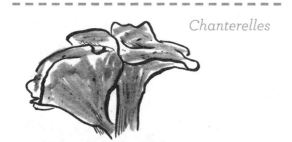

**Chanterelles.** From summer into fall, look for these bright orange or yellow, trumpet-shaped mushrooms in loose groups at the foot of hardwood trees. Some people say that fresh chanterelles have a fruity fragrance. Their texture can be chewy, but it softens nicely when cooked for a long time at a low temperature, which makes them well-suited to eating in soups and stews.

**Boletes.** You may find any of the more than 200 different species of boletes common in North America. They have rounded tops with thick stems and can be up to ten inches tall and ten inches across the cap. The tops of the caps are usually brown or reddish-brown, and the pores underneath can be whitish, yellow, brown, orange, or red. Ditch any that are orange or red—they may be mildly poisonous and definitely don't taste good. Eat only the caps and be sure to cook them first. Boletes come up in summer and fall, often near pine trees.

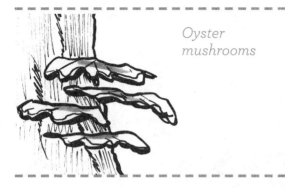

*Oyster mushrooms*

**Oyster mushrooms.** The trunks of living trees and fallen logs host oyster mushrooms, which grow in clusters clinging to the bark. They're white or tan and reach up to eight inches across. Oyster mushrooms show up after wet weather almost all year long, but especially in late fall. Little black beetles sometimes infest oyster mushrooms, so soak them in salt water before you cook them to get rid of the bugs.

**Hen-of-the-woods.** A big ruffled fungus that can look like a chicken, hen-of-the-woods forms on stumps and fallen logs, often in the same spot year after year. They can be very big—up to 100 pounds—but you want to eat only the freshest growth because it is the most tender part. Cook it slowly for a long time to get the best flavor and texture.

*Hen of the Woods*

# CHAPTER THREE:

# SAVE IT FOR LATER

**P**eople on the move need food that travels. So early hunters and gatherers started figuring out ways to keep food they couldn't eat right away from spoiling. Today, wherever you go you can always find food—anytime, day or night, in convenience stores, pharmacies, and mega-centers. But much of the food is loaded with an alphabet soup of preservatives to give it years of shelf-life, though they may shorten ours.

So you're not a nomad (except for those months when you couch-surfed after college) or living on the frontier where there are no stores. Why, then, would you want to preserve food yourself? Number one, because it's the only way to eat and serve homegrown and local food all year long, no matter what climate you live in. You will always be able to eat food that is healthy, real, and free of artificial preservatives. Putting up your own food, as the old-timers used to say, is fun to do and leaves you with that great feeling you get from being prepared for anything.

Storing fresh food can be very simple and, for many foods, almost labor-free. The basic techniques of dehydrating, freezing, and cellaring require no special equipment. In this chapter I will share with you the know-how you need to get started. Canning is more exacting and time-consuming, but once you understand the principles, you will be on your way to the very satisfying sight of your pantry full of gleaming jars of fruits and vegetables. Even if you don't have a pantry or much storage space at all, you can preserve food and, with the suggestions I've come up with and your own ingenuity, find room to keep it.

## BEST FOR DRYING

| | |
|---|---|
| Apples | Meat |
| Grapes | Onions |
| Herbs | Tomatoes |
| Hot peppers | |

# Dehydrating

**The easiest and least space-inten-**sive way to preserve food, dehydration just kind of happens. The results can be fun (as in "fruit leather"), chic (sundried tomatoes), practical (jerky), and handy (herbs). Dehydration is just what it sounds like: drying the fluids out of the food. This has a significant impact because fruits and vegetables range from 80 to 95% water volume. Dehydration helps the food last longer because bacteria grow in the water and then cause the food to spoil. If you have limited storage space, dehydrated food is convenient because it keeps at room temperature and takes up little room.

Though food dehydrates gradually on its own, you want to manage the process to get the best results. Air-drying is simple, but unless you live in a very hot, low-humidity climate, it's feasible for only a few foods. For most of the juicier fruits and vegetables, a dedicated food dehydrator or your kitchen's oven are more effective at drying them out evenly.

No matter what food you plan to dehydrate, if you are harvesting it from your garden, pick it early in the day you are going to preserve it—after the dew has dried off but before the sun has heated it up. Slightly underripe produce is better than overripe, because food past its prime may already have microbes growing on it that may cause it to rot in storage. For the same reason, don't preserve food that is bruised or has even a little mold growing on it. Rinse the food thoroughly to remove any soil or insects, and then drain it as well as you can—you want the drying process to remove the moisture inside without water outside to slow the dehydration or become a host to mold.

Any way you plan to dehydrate the

food—using dry air, a dehydrator, or an oven—air circulation is critical to even, thorough drying. Placing the food on a rack during the process allows air to flow around it. You can buy dehydration trays or make your own with ordinary oven racks or the grid-type used by bakers to let cakes cool. Wrap the racks with cheesecloth or synthetic mesh netting, stretched tightly and held fast with clothespins or the metal binder clips found in office supply stores. Many do-it-yourselfers use galvanized window screening for drying food. Avoid using screens because they have been treated with zinc and cadmium, and acidic (such as tomatoes) foods may react with them and cause heavy metals to get into your food. Stick to food-grade metal racks.

When putting food on racks to dry, spread it out and don't let the pieces touch each other. You want to be sure there is plenty of room around each piece so that air can circulate. Turn it every few hours so that all sides dry evenly. After the food is dehydrated, store it in tightly sealed jars or resealable bags. Keep the containers in a cool, dry place that's sheltered from direct sunlight. Dehydrated food typically keeps for six months to one year. You can reconstitute dried food by soaking it in room-temperature water for a half hour. Use it in any recipe that calls for a frozen or canned ingredient.

## AIR-DRYING

The most critical factors for drying fruits and vegetables are temperature, circulation, and humidity. To air-dry effectively, you need two to three days of daytime temperatures in the low nineties and humidity less than 80%, with nighttime temperatures remaining in the seventies. If the temperatures are expected to drop lower overnight, bring the trays inside and put them back out the next morning. The hot, dry conditions are critical because when the temperature is too low at the start of dehydration, destructive microbes survive and spoil the food before it's finished drying. Direct sunlight cooks the surface of the food and hardens the outer skin, trapping moisture inside.

The best spot to air-dry food is away from direct sunlight but with steady airflow—a covered porch or balcony is ideal. One unexpected place that can work for air-drying is your car. On a sunny summer day, the inside of your car can be ten or more degrees warmer than outside. It can get hot and dry enough to dehydrate even tomatoes in a single day. Leave all the windows cracked to allow fresh air to circulate. Be extra careful not to let the juices that leak as the food dries drip onto your seats or floor mats.

That's sure to hurt the car's resale value! Wherever you put the trays, cover them with cheesecloth or a very thin fabric that allows air and moisture to pass through while keeping bugs and debris off the food.

Air-drying works best for herbs and a few unique vegetables—most other food won't yield appetizing or even safe results. (In fact, most "sun-dried tomatoes" you find at supermarkets are dehydrated in factory-scale ovens.) Starting on page 99 I'll cover how to dehydrate lots of other foods using an electric food dryer or your oven. But first I'll explain what you can air-dry and how.

## HERBS

Air-drying works so well for herbs that you can even air-dry them inside your home. It's the best way to retain their colors and essential oils—the source of their flavor and fragrance. Rosemary, thyme, oregano, dill, parsley, and lavender top the list of easiest herbs to air-dry. (Basil is much better preserved in pesto than dehydrated.)

When harvesting your homegrown herbs, cut the branches before the plants flower— the flavor and aroma diminish as they mature. You want branches that are six to eight inches long. Whether you get herbs from your garden or the farmer's market, you start out with bunches, but when they've dried you're left with the small amounts you need to add authentic flavor to any dish.

The best way to dry herbs is slightly different than with fruits and vegetables. You put them in paper lunch bags instead of on trays while they're drying. The steps are simple.

1. Label each bag with the name of the herb you will put in it. Poke a few small holes about two-thirds of the way up on both sides of each bag. Grab four to six herb stems in a bundle and place the bag over the herbs. Gather the ends of the bag around the stems and tie it closed with twine.

2. Hang the bagged herb bundle upside down in a well-ventilated room with low humidity. You can use just about any room in your house—closets and attics work well because you have rods or beams where you can hang the bags. Belowground basements tend to be damper than other rooms, so they're not ideal for drying herbs.

3. After two weeks open a couple of the bags and touch the leaves. If they are crispy and crumble easily between your fingers, they are sufficiently dry. (If they're not, retie the bags closed and check again weekly until they are.)

4. When you're ready to use the dried herbs, you get the strongest and freshest flavor if you store them whole and crumble the leaves as you use them. Dried herbs have concentrated flavors, so you don't need as much as you do with fresh. In recipes that call for fresh herbs, use one-quarter to one-third of the amount of dried herbs for the same taste. Your dehydrated herbs will last for about a year before the essential oil—and the flavor and fragrance—has faded.

## PEPPERS

Chiles, especially the small, fiery ones, air-dry quickly on late summer days when they're ripe. After they've dried, you can keep the peppers whole and add them, as I do, to homemade chili in the winter. You also can grind them up in a food processor (or even a coffee grinder) to make hot pepper flakes you can sprinkle on pizza and other foods you'd like to spice up.

The traditional method of preserving and storing chile peppers is to weave them into a *ristra*, or strand, that hangs in your kitchen. Well-crafted ristras are decorative and make efficient use of your space for storing food.

1. All you need to make a ristra is a few dozen or more ripe red chiles and twine. You don't want to use green (unripe) chiles because they are not fully mature and shrivel up before they're dry. Pick bright red pods and set them in a cool, shaded, well-ventilated area for a few days to start drying first.

2. When the stems have started to turn from green to brown, take three of them and wrap twine twice around the stems. Pull the string up between two of the peppers, and pull tight. Tie the string into a half hitch and loop it around all three stems; pull the string tight.

3. Make another cluster of three chile pods and tie it about three inches above the first. Continue until you have six or seven clusters of peppers. Break the string and start again. Start tying the same way and continue until you have used all of the chiles. You can tie a loop in the loose end of the twine or knot a short, thin wooden dowel at the end to keep the clusters from slipping off.

4. Starting with two of the strings, weave a long piece of twine through each of the clusters. As you weave, turn the clusters to face in alternate directions so that the strand hangs balanced when you are done.

5. Hang the ristra outside where the peppers

continue air-drying—as always, in a spot out of direct sun, where air circulates freely. If you have no place to put it outside, you can hang it inside, but be sure to put a few sheets of newspaper underneath it, because as the peppers are drying, they drip red juice that stains. Depending on your climate, the peppers will be thoroughly dry in two to four weeks. During the process and after, imme- diately remove any pods that start to look moldy so they don't spoil others.

**6.** As you're ready to use the peppers, snip them off the strand from the bottom. I've kept a ristra for a couple of years, but the peppers seem to lose their punch after a year or so.

Though garlic and onions don't dehydrate fully like peppers do this way, you can store them in a similar fashion by weaving them into braids. You need the aboveground leaves that grow atop onions or garlic to do this, so you'll need to grow them yourself or get them from a farmer who's left the leaves on.

Start by letting the bulbs "cure" for a couple weeks, so they become less juicy and the leaves change from yellow to brown. After brushing (not washing!) off any dirt left on the bulbs, wrap the leaves of three bulbs over and under each other into a tight weave. When you have six or seven clusters, wrap twine between and around the woven leaves to tie them together and form a braid that's a foot to a foot and half long.

If you want to show off your handiwork by hanging your allium (botanist's word for onions, garlic, and the like) braid or ristra around your kitchen, put it in a place away from the cooking area—even occasional exposure to steam will cause them to rot. But remember they're not just décor—eat and enjoy them throughout the year.

## ONIONS

Though onions are moister than peppers, you can air-dry them—just not whole. Yellow and white "storage" varieties such as Copra and Yellow Globe start off drier than other types of onions. Whichever kind you use, first slice them into pieces about a quarter-inch thick. They air-dry quickly into flakes you can add to any dish calling for a bit of onion flavor. Or grind them into onion powder for sprinkling into soups, tomato sauce, or other food.

## HEAT DRYING

You can dry a lot of other foods in a dedicated food dehydrator or an oven (even a toaster oven), a process I'll call heat drying. Tomatoes come out great from a dehydrator, and you can also dry zucchini and peas this way. Even better, fruit such as apples and pears, berries and grapes, apricots, plums, and peaches all heat-dry into tasty, chewy snacks you can eat alone or in a mix with nuts and other good stuff. You also can make your own fruit leather with heat drying, too.

You can find lots of models of dehydra-

**Small Space Project**

USING PASSIVE SOLAR POWER TO DEHYDRATE FOOD IS ENERGY-EFFICIENT AND lets you dry tomatoes and fruit for which air-drying typically isn't fast enough. You can make this simple solar food dehydrator with stuff you have around the house or that's easy to scrounge up. It's better to try drying on a sunny day, in warm but not scalding temperatures, rather than in the dead of winter.

**1.** Get a long, shallow cardboard box like a men's shirt box or gift box. The lid will be the solar panel, and the food will go inside the bottom half of the box.

**2.** Cut four air holes in each of the narrow ends of the box's top piece—the holes should be about the size of a bottle cap.

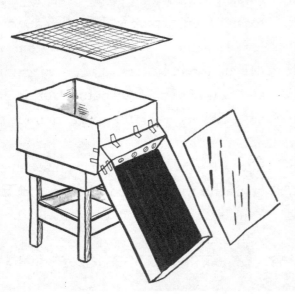

**3.** Paint the inside of the top black, or line it with a black plastic bag.

**4.** Cover the top with clear plastic. This section captures heat from the sun, which will be reflected back on the food.

**5.** Cut matching holes in one end of the bottom piece of the box.

**6.** Place the two boxes so that one set of holes on the top lines up with the holes on the bottom. Then, using scrap cardboard and masking tape, form an air duct that guides the air flow from the lid (the solar collector side) into the bottom section, where the food is.

**7.** Set the drying box (the bottom) on a stool

or stand and lean the solar box (the top) against the stool at the most effective angle to catch the sun's rays.

8. Spread a piece of cheesecloth or other thin fabric on top of the drying box. Put the food you want to dehydrate on the cloth or screen. If the sunlight is steady all day, the food should be ready for storage by sundown.

tors with a variety of features, but almost all of them have stackable trays, a small warming device, and a fan. Different types of trays (or inserts) are very helpful if you want to make fruit leather or jerky. The most efficient models have the heating element and the fan at the back rather than the bottom of the dehydrator, but those units tend to be smaller. A generation or two back, food dehydrators were as common for wedding gifts as fondue pots were. You may be able to pick one up that's been barely used at a yard sale or flea market.

Standard and toaster ovens can work as food dehydrators, too. You need to set them at their lowest temperature so the food doesn't cook before it's dry. Ovens have drawbacks that make them less than ideal for drying food. Unless they have a convection setting, they have no fan to circulate the heated air. That slows the process down, which means you may need to leave your oven on for a whole day, which you'll probably notice on your utility bill. Ovens can handle only a couple of trays at a time—a toaster oven even fewer—in contrast to the stacked-type dehydrator that can have six or more trays drying at the same time. Your microwave isn't a good alternative—even at the lowest setting the food will cook. You can use an oven to dry food, but if you get serious about it, a dedicated food dehydrator is a worthwhile investment.

## DRYING SAFELY

*Caution:* You cannot break up the heat-drying process into multiple sessions. Once you start dehydrating, don't let the food cool down until it is fully dry. Mold, bacteria, and other spoilers grow on partially dried food.

1. Blanching before you preserve food kills the microbes that cause rot. (See "Blanche du Vegetable" on page 119 for details on how to do this.) Dehydrated tomatoes last longer if you blanch them first. For the same reason and results, treat fresh fruit with an antioxidant such as ascorbic acid instead of blanching before you dry it (see page 105).

2. When drying tomatoes or larger fruits, slice them into pieces about a half-inch thick (definitely no thicker), so they can dry evenly and completely. Remove cores, seeds, and any other inedible parts before drying.

3. When your fruit or vegetables are ready to be dehydrated, spread them out on the trays—remember to leave room around each item for heat and air to circulate—and set the temperature at 140°F. After two to three hours (depending on how juicy the food was to start), the food will have "sweated" out much of the moisture. The flesh will have begun to pucker and the sides to curl up. Reduce the temperature to 120°F; the gradual drying will continue without causing the food to shrivel up or cook. Well-designed new dehydrators adjust the temperature at this stage automatically with an internal thermostat, but you have to pay attention to this yourself if you are using an ordinary oven or an older dehydrator.

4. Throughout the process, rotate the trays in your dehydrator or oven every four hours or so to be sure they are all drying evenly. At that time, flip the slices of food so they dry equally on both sides.

5. With heat drying, fruits and vegetables fully dehydrate in four to twelve hours, depending on the type of food. No matter how long the dehydration process is taking, resist the temptation to speed it up by turning the temperature higher. If you do, the food develops a scorched flavor or may even burn up. Check on the food you're drying every couple hours and, if it is shriveling away, take it out of the dryer or oven.

6. After four hours, press or squeeze the fruits and vegetables to see if moisture beads up on the skin. If so, continue drying. When you don't see water beads anymore and the food feels dry to your touch, it's done and ready for long-term storage.

## FRUIT LEATHER

The chewy blend of corn syrup, thickeners, and artificial flavors that's sold in stores as "fruit snacks" is a pale comparison to real fruit leathers. Making your own with real fruit is easy if you have a food dehydrator. Most models come with or you can order extra a tray designed for making fruit leather. You can also make fruit leather in your oven. You can make fruit leather from apples and pears, peaches and apricots, cherries and all kinds of berries, or a combination of all of them.

**1.** Wash, destem, core, and/or pit four to five pounds of fruit. If necessary, cut it up into pieces that will fit into a blender or food processor.

**2.** Puree the fruit with a cup or so of unsweetened applesauce. The fruit is naturally sweet, but you can add honey, maple syrup, or ordinary sugar, if you want. Two and half cups of puree makes a sheet of dried fruit about the size of a baking tray.

3. Preheat your dehydrator or get your oven to 140°F. Coat the tray or a baking sheet very lightly with a nonstick spray or oil, then pour the puree onto it. Tilt the tray a bit in each direction to spread the puree evenly. Put the tray in the oven or dehydrator. When using an oven, leave the oven door open slightly to allow moisture to escape.

4. Drying fruit leather takes six to twelve hours, depending on the fruit and how much fluid is in the puree. The leather is ready when it is solid and stretches a bit when you pull on it.

5. While it is still a bit warm, roll it up or cut it into strips. Wrap in wax paper and store in air-tight plastic bags or containers. Fruit leather can stay in a cool, dry place like your pantry for a week or two. For longer storage, keep in your refrigerator or freezer.

## ARRESTING OXIDATION

WHEN APPLES, PEACHES, PEARS, APRICOTS, OR OTHER LIGHT-COLORED FRUITS are cut and exposed to the air, their flesh starts turning brown almost right away. This is caused by oxidation, and if you don't stop it, the fruit will look, smell, and taste less appealing when you preserve it.

A simple solution you can make yourself with ascorbic acid, which you can find in most drugstores, stops the oxidation process. To treat five quarts of fruit, mix one to two teaspoons of ascorbic acid in a cup of water. Sprinkle the solution onto cut fruit and stir lightly so that all of the pieces are well coated. Drain off any excess before you dry or freeze these fresh fruits.

## JERKY JOY

If you or someone you know hunts, or if you just like to have a little animal protein handy for camping trips, late nights at the office, or unexpected dinner guests, drying meat for jerky is simple to do and gives you a chance to be a little creative.

Fats are the first thing to spoil, so start with the leanest meats. Venison, elk, and other game meats work well because they are nat-urally low in fat. If you go with beef, use cuts like sirloin, tenderloin, and top round, and pass on tougher or fattier flank steak or brisket. Figure that four pounds of fresh meat becomes one pound of dried jerky.

Cleanliness is next to healthfulness when you are working with meat. Before you start, thoroughly clean your hands, utensils, and the work surface. Use a food dehydrator rather than your oven for making jerky.

1. With a sharp knife, trim off the meat any visible sections of fat and any cartilage or membrane attached to it. Cut the meat into thin strips—about six inches long and a quarter-inch thick. Cut across the grain of the meat for the best drying surface. Hint: Raw meat generally is easier to cut when it's hardened—though still pliable—from being slightly frozen.

2. Marinate the meat before you dry it to infuse it with flavors that you like. Go Asian or Southwest, classic American or your own invention. Whichever taste you choose, use about a half-cup of marinade for each pound of meat. Coat each strip well with the marinade, put them in a glass or ceramic container, cover it, and leave in your refrigerator for at least eight hours.

3. After the strips of meat have marinated, spread them out on a tray in a single layer with as much space around each as possible. Meat, especially after it's been marinated, drips a lot in the early stages of dehydrating.

Cover the trays with foil so the drippings don't dry on the trays.

4. Preheat the oven or set the dehydrator to 120°F. Put the rack in the middle of the oven. Leave the door slightly ajar, if you can, so moisture can escape faster.

5. The jerky is fully dehydrated and ready to eat or store when it bends slightly and then breaks. Depending on the type of meat and the size of the strips, the jerky dries in about twelve hours in a dehydrator or twenty-four hours in the oven.

6. Let the jerky cool thoroughly. Check it again to be sure it bends and then breaks.

7. Jerky exists to last longer than fresh meat, but it still slowly deteriorates if you don't store it sensibly. Keep it for a week at room temperature in a resealable plastic bag or glass jar. To store it for longer periods, refrigerate it. In the freezer it keeps for about a year.

## SMOKED FISH

You know how fast fresh seafood spoils—like the old Benjamin Franklin saying goes, visitors and fish start to stink after three days. I don't know what to do about the guests, but you can preserve fish and enjoy it for months after by soaking it in salt water and exposing it to smoke from a fire. The process adds flavor to the fish, too. Whether you catch your own or buy fresh fish you want to preserve, all you need is a smoker (similar to a small backyard grill) and wood to burn, and you can use the preservation method people have depended upon for thousands of years. Many people already own smokers for beef, pork, or chicken: it's a great way to make meat extra tender and flavorful, but it won't preserve the meat as it does fish.

This technique works with any kind of fish, but the fattier the fish, the better it will absorb smoke and the longer it will last. Trout and salmon are two popular choices, though sturgeon and sablefish work well, too. If you catch the fish yourself, pack them in ice right away and clean them just before you're ready to smoke them.

Your ordinary backyard grill is designed to cook food with heat from the coals or flames. Smokers look a lot like grills, but they keep the food away from direct heat so that smoke can saturate the food. Many models have a pan of water set between the food and the heat, moderating the temperature and increasing the volume of smoke. Whichever model you get, be sure it has a tight-fitting lid and is sealed well all around. Prices for a smoker range from $300 for a very a basic model to $3,000 for a full-featured, top-of-the-line model. You may be able to find a functioning used smoker at a garage sale or flea market for less than a hundred bucks.

Hardwoods like oak or hickory burn slower and more evenly than softwoods such as pine or spruce: stick with hardwoods for your smoker. You can impart subtle flavor to the fish by using aromatic wood, such apple, cherry, cedar, or mesquite. If you don't have access to seasoned (well-dried) wood, you can use bagged charcoal in a smoker.

You can smoke fish in a matter of hours at a relatively high temperature, but the fish would need to be consumed within a few days. That's "hot" smoking. To preserve fish for longer, a longer cooking time at a lower temperature is the secret. "Cold-smoked" fish keeps in the refrigerator for a few months.

1. Prepare the fish: rinse it thoroughly in clean water and, if it's whole, remove the head, tail, backbone, and guts. You can remove the skin now, if you want, but it comes off much more easily after smoking. Cut the fish into large equal-size pieces for brining—brining times are based on weight per piece, and each piece should brine evenly. One-pound portions are about right.

2. Mix the brine: in a large bowl, mix three and a half cups of salt (noniodized, like kosher or sea salt) in a gallon of water. Mix well until all of the salt has dissolved. You can substitute red wine for some of the water, if you like the flavor in your fish. Add seasonings such as peppercorns, garlic cloves, or dill sprigs to the brine. Many experienced smokers also add a bit of brown sugar to the brine: up to half the amount of salt used. Salt and the sugar draw moisture out of the fish as it soaks up their flavor. You need a gallon of brine for every four pounds of fish.

3. Put the fish in a large flat plastic, ceramic, or glass dish and pour in the brine. Each piece of fish should be fully submerged in the brine. Cover, and store the dish in the refrigerator while the fish soaks. The fish should soak in the brine for about an hour and fifteen minutes per pound—that's not total weight, but the weight of each piece. So if you have four one-pound pieces, they should soak in brine for an hour and fifteen minutes. If you have one four-pound piece, you leave it in the brine for five hours. If you have removed the skin from the fish, brine for only about an hour per pound.

4. When the brining is finished, you don't have to rinse the fish—it's your choice—but if left unwashed, the smoked fish will have a saltier flavor when it's done. Whether you rinse or not, the fish needs to dry well after brining and before smoking: place the fish skin-side down on smoker racks, and put the racks in a cool spot out of direct sun and with

steady airflow. If you don't have a spot with good circulation, set up a small electric fan to blow around (though not at) the fish to provide a breeze while keeping insects away from the fish. Be sure they're out of the reach of any household pets. After two to three hours of drying, you'll see a shiny glaze form on the fish. The glaze, called the "pellicle," helps seal moisture inside the fish, so it stays tender and flaky through the smoking process, and it absorbs the smoky flavor. You'll know the pellicle has formed when the fish's flesh feels slightly tacky when you touch it.

**5.** There are two cooking methods: cold and hot smoking. Hot smoking is actually more of a cooking process than it is a preservation technique, though hot-smoked fish keeps in the refrigerator for a few days after. Preparing the fish this way keeps it moister than if you grill it. To hot-smoke fish, you want the smoker no warmer than 90°F for the first two hours, helping to complete the pellicle before you increase the temperature. After a couple of hours at 90°F, stoke the smoker up to 180°F, but no higher or you risk completely cooking the fish. An inch-thick piece of fish (about half a pound in weight) takes about six hours to finish hot smoking. (Extend the smoking time for thicker pieces of fish.) You'll know when it's finished when the fish is golden in color and flaky when pressed with a fork.

**6.** For cold-smoking, and to truly preserve fish, smoke it continuously in the smoker at a lower temperature for five days. The fish is prepared the same way as you do with hot smoking, but do not raise the temperature after the first two hours (ideally it should be maintained at 80°F). Keep the smoker going day and night for five days: if you're burning hardwood logs, check on the fire about three times a day. The fish is done when it is very brown on the outside and the flesh is noticeably dry, firm, and sliceable. The fish will last, refrigerated, for several months.

**7.** Let the smoked fish cool completely on its rack before eating it or storing it in a sealed container in your refrigerator or freezer.

# *Freezing*

## BEST FOR FREEZING

| | |
|---|---|
| Asparagus | Broccoli |
| Beans | Pesto |
| Berries | Sweet peppers |

**The quickest and coolest way to** preserve food (as in least hot, which is no trifle after a long day in the sun) is to freeze it. A storage or chest freezer makes it easy to keep a lot of food for months, but even if you have just the freezer attached to your refrigerator, you can store a few of your favorite fruits and vegetables to enjoy when their growing season is over.

As you can tell from a stroll down the frozen food aisle at the supermarket, a variety of fruits and vegetables keep well in cold storage. Soft, leafy greens such as lettuce and spinach don't stand up well to freezing, nor do cucumbers, watermelon, and other foods with a very high water content.

After you harvest the food you want to freeze from your garden or bring it home from the farmer's market, rinse it well to wash away any dirt or tiny bugs that came along for the ride. Even more important, be sure that the food is completely dry before you put it in the freezer. Any water clinging to the food forms ice in the freezer and can spoil the texture when you are ready to eat it.

Plastic freezer bags are the most space-efficient containers for storing frozen food. To protect the food from freezer "burn," which leaves behind unpleasant flavors, be sure the bags have no holes, that you press all the air out after you put the food in, and that the seal is tight. Label the bags clearly with both the name of the item inside and the date you freeze it. If the food is dry when frozen and the bags are well sealed, you can enjoy it for up to a year later. Defrosting the food before you eat it often leaves it soggy. Better to start cooking with it while it's still frozen.

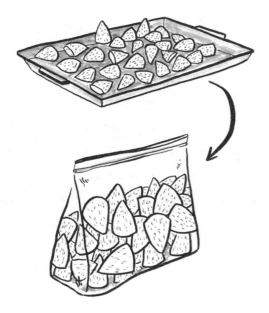

put them in the bag keeps them from turning into one big clump. With this approach, you can pull out as much as you want to add to batter for pancakes or muffins, or to prepare for pie filling.

Sweet peppers are almost as easy to store in the freezer. Cut them into strips, then freeze them on a tray, just as described for berries—in a single layer, not touching. When they're frozen solid, combine them all in a freezer bag. They won't come out of the freezer as crisp and juicy as they are when you eat them on a salad in summer, but they'll be perfect for using on pizzas, in stir-fries, or sautéed with onions for omelets, sandwiches, and burritos. You can freeze chile (hot) peppers this way, too, but they keep so well when they're dried that you don't need to use freezer space for them.

Asparagus, broccoli, beans, cauliflower, and peas (with and without edible pods) take a few extra steps before you freeze them, but they all keep well in cold storage. Clean them well and prep them as if you were going to eat them right away. That is, remove leaves, stems, pods, or

Berries, especially blueberries and raspberries, could not be easier to get ready for freezer storage. Remove any stems or leaves that you picked along with berries, rinse lightly, and let the berries dry on a paper towel. When the berries are fully dry, spread them out in a single layer on a baking sheet or other tray. Don't crowd them so that they are touching—do several batches, if necessary. Put the tray in your freezer for at least twelve hours, then take it out and pour the frozen berries into a freezer bag. Freezing them before you other inedible parts, then cut them into bite-size pieces. Then you want to blanch them according to the directions on page 119. After the vegetables are blanched and completely dry again, spread the pieces onto baking sheets or other trays and put them in the freezer overnight. Put only enough for one meal or serving in each bag.

Sweet corn is one of the most beloved flavors of summer, so many people want to preserve it in the freezer. I've tried a lot of frozen corn on the cob, and it never has the same crisp squirt-when-you-bite-into-a-kernel texture when it's fresh off the stalk. You can freeze corn right on the cob—some people just stick the ears in freezer bags with the husk still on. But the corn gets mushy—because the cob retains water—and the ears clearly take up a lot of freezer space. So I think you're better off freezing just the kernels and waiting until next summer for another chance to munch your way back and forth on a fresh ear. To freeze sweet corn, blanch it while still on the cob, then scrape off the kernels into your storage bags. Again, put just

enough for one meal or serving in a bag.

Tomatoes, whole or cut into chunks, store in the freezer without blanching. Frozen tomatoes are best used in soups, stews, sauces, and the like because freezing breaks their texture down completely and they become mushy. Also, the skins can get tough in storage, so loosen them by running hot water over the tomatoes and then peeling back the skin before freezing. No need to freeze tomatoes on trays, but do pack them into single-serving bags so you can take out only what you need when you are ready to use them—there's no way to separate them at that time. Even better, cook the tomatoes into a sauce or paste and then freeze that.

Herbs do not freeze well whole, but you can preserve the flavor of fresh basil by making it into pesto and then pouring it into an empty ice cube tray. Once solid, you can pop the pesto cubes out of the tray and store them in plastic bags in your freezer until you're ready to eat them with pasta or other dishes.

# Canning

**If your grandmother or great-** grandmother canned fruits and vegetables, she probably did it out of necessity. For most people, it was the only way to have produce to eat all year long. The technology of industrial food canning has progressed so that today's canned vegetables are much more appealing than the mushy peas and carrots out of the tin that I grew up with in the 1960s.

No one living in North America in the twenty-first century needs to depend on food they've canned themselves. And yet, canning is enjoying an unexpected revival, with canning classes and even canning parties attracting crowds of people who want to put up the food they've grown, picked, or bought at the farmer's market. Canning Across America is an organization dedicated to teaching about and encouraging food preservation with an information-filled Web site that lists events, recipes, and resources. (Check it out at www.canningacross america.com.)

You might attribute this resurgent interest in canning to fears about Biphenol A, a component of a resin used to coat the inside of aluminum and tin food cans that may leach into the food. BPA is linked with developmental and reproductive disorders and cancers. But I think that today's canners enjoy the experience of doing it for themselves, and they get genuine satisfaction from opening a jar of food they put up themselves and remembering the effort they made to preserve it.

But before you start canning, you need to be aware that drying and freezing food are very forgiving processes. You need to follow basic guidelines, but there's plenty of room for interpretation. It's cooking at its most basic—once you have the steps down, you can vary the formula a bit to your taste and experience. Canning, however, is more like baking because you work with a formula that you must follow or you risk ending up with useless results. And when you make a mistake with canning, you can get you and your family very sick.

That risk is why the U.S. Department of Agriculture has studied and published specific instructions for canning each type of fruit or vegetable. You must adhere to them strictly. You can get this information from your cooperative extension agent or from the National Center for Home Food Preservation (at www.uga.edu/nchfp). I'll introduce you to the basics of canning here, but you still need to get key details from the USDA and other tested canning recipes.

The safest way to can your own food is with a pressure canner, a large pot with a tight-fighting lid that uses high heat and pressure to kill botulism, mold, yeasts, and other undesirable organisms in food. Boiling-water canners generally cost less and work faster, but they're safely used only for already cooked foods, like tomato sauce, jams, and jellies. Boiling water canning is not safe for low-acid foods, as most vegetables (except tomatoes) are, because the botulism bacteria may survive without the addition of pressure to the heat. Don't try processing canning jars in an oven, microwave, or dishwasher (yes, it gets hot in there!). You can't safely manage the conditions to the exact specifications.

With a pressure canner, you can pack raw food into the jars. But "raw-packing" can leave air trapped in and around the food, which may cause it to discolor after a few months of storage. Hot-packing, in which you simmer the food in boiling water for two to five minutes (depending on the food and the size of the pieces) before pouring it into the jars, is more reliable. Cooking helps remove air from the food and, at the same time, softens it so you can fit more into each jar. Just as important, the precooked food will look and taste better when you open the jar. For your first couple attempts at canning, I suggest you stick with hot-packing—it's much less risky.

Headspace is critical, too. I'm not talking about what your stoner neighbor needs when he's having a bummer of a day. No, this is about how much room you leave when filling canning jars with food. Without enough headspace, the food will be forced out of the jar when you seal it, which is more than just a mess in the canner. Food that winds up outside on the jar's rim or around the lid can harbor mold, which can break a seal and cause the canned food to spoil. Too much headspace leaves air inside the jar that can also cause it to go bad.

Most vegetables and fruits—either in pint or quart jars—need about a half-inch of headspace, but don't assume that is always true. Headspace requirements change with the density, shape, and cooking characteristics of individual foods. The USDA has developed and disseminated headspace guidelines for each kind of food so you get this exactly right. Follow headspace the USDA's directions exactly and be sure to measure the space carefully—too much headspace can make it more difficult to seal jars.

I'm all for reusing and recycling, but empty mayonnaise and peanut butter jars won't work for canning. You need jars with a mouth designed to create a tight seal with a canning lid. These "mason" jars cost about seventy-five cents to a dollar each and come in a variety of sizes. You may find used mason jars at yard sales or flea markets. If they have no cracks or chips, you can use them. Wide-mouth jars are easiest to fill.

Canning jars are closed with two-piece tops—a flat metal lid shaped like a disk (rimmed with a rubber gasket called a "flange") that covers the jar opening, and a screw-on band that holds the lid in place. Never reuse the flat metal lids once they've been processed in water once, but you can reuse the screw-on bands, as long as they fit tightly and aren't rusty.

## CANNING STEPS

*Clean and sterilize.* Thoroughly wash the bands, lids, and jars in hot, soapy water—either by hand or in the dishwasher. Then sterilize the lids by boiling them in water for ten minutes. Remove the pan from the heat but leave the tops in hot water until you're ready to use them.

*Pick and prepare.* Use your youngest, most tender fruits and vegetables for canning. It's especially critical when you are canning to skip those that are overripe or blemished. Harvest just before you're ready to can to keep the produce from losing nutrients. Wash each item well and cut them into serving-size pieces, if necessary. Contact with bowls, cookware, or utensils made of aluminum, copper, iron, or chipped enamel may cause the food to discolor once it is canned, so avoid those materials during your preparation.

*Fill and cap.* With a large spoon or ladle, put the produce into jars. (A canning funnel comes in handy here but is not crucial.) Then fill the jars with boiling water, pickling solution (for pickles), or sweet syrup or white grape juice (for fruit). The food expands during the canning process, which is why you need the headspace, or room between the contents and the top of the jar. With a small silicone spatula, push down on the produce in each jar to submerge it under the liquid; then run the spatula along the inside of the jar to eliminate air bubbles. A chopstick also works well to find air bubbles. Next, use a damp paper towel to clean off the jar rims. Close each jar with a lid and a metal band, and screw the bands on fingertip tight; don't force them any tighter than they go with a moderate twist.

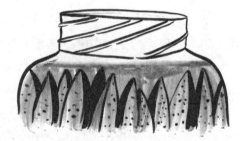

*Load the canner.* Put filled, capped jars into a canning rack and then lower the rack into the canner by its handles, or use a jar lifter to insert individual jars into a rack that's already in place in the pot.

Position the jars in the canner so that they are not touching.

**Heat thoroughly.** If you're using a pressure canner, follow the manufacturer's directions, which will vary depending on the type of canner and the altitude. Generally, fill the pressure canner with two inches of hot water, add the jars, put the lid on the pot, and achieve the directed pressure before you start tracking processing time. Once you can maintain the correct pressure without adjusting the heat, you can follow the recommended processing time for the recipe. If the pressure drops, stop timing and adjust, then resume timing. Be sure to look up any processing adjustments you may need for a high altitude. When processing is finished, remove the pot from the heat and let the pressure drop before opening the canner and removing the jars.

**Cool and check.** Use jar lifters to gently remove the jars from the canner and place them an inch apart on a wooden board to cool. While they cool, the lid gaskets become firmly sealed to the jars. After twenty-four hours, check the lids to be sure they are airtight. Press down with your finger on each metal lid. It should not go down or spring back up. Double-check the seals by tapping each lid with a teaspoon, and listen for a high-pitched ping, not a thud. The ping indicates the seal is tight. Put any unsealed jar in your refrigerator, and eat the contents in the next few days. Wipe off any food on the outside of the sealed jars, and label them with the contents and the date you sealed them. Sealed jars can be stored without the metal bands.

**Safe storage.** You have every reason to be proud of your home-canned jars, so I understand why you want to display them around your kitchen. Put a few of them where they will be seen. But jars are best kept in a cool, dark, dry place. If you don't have room in your pantry or in a basement, see "Hidden Storage" on page 121.

## BLANCH DU VEGETABLE

WHEN YOU LEARN ABOUT PRESERVING FOOD, YOU HEAR A LOT ABOUT BLANCHING. You need to realize that as soon as you pick a fruit, vegetable, or herb off the plant, enzymes are activated that cause the color, flavor, texture and nutrient levels to start changing. You can deactivate the enzymes with heat: a super-quick boiling or steaming process called blanching. If you try to freeze or can most foods without blanching them, they're very likely to turn into a mushy, unappealing mess when you are ready to eat them.

Blanching sounds like a complicated, advanced cooking technique, but it really isn't. Here's what you need to know.

**1.** Fill a large pot half-full with water, and stir in a quarter-teaspoon of citric acid for each quart of water. (Citric acid acts as an anti-darkening and antimicrobial agent.) Bring the water to a boil.

**2.** In the meantime, fill another pot with ice water, and have a bowl of ice cubes handy so that you can keep the water cold.

**3.** Cut one dry quart of vegetables into bite-size pieces. You can put them in a wire basket that fits fully into the pot or put them in a cheesecloth or other mesh bag that you twist-tie closed.

**4.** Submerge the vegetables in boiling water so that all the vegetables are covered with water. Start timing as soon as the vegetables go into the water. (The water should return to boiling within a minute—if not, you are using too much vegetable for the amount of water.) You can get exact timing for how long each vegetable you are blanching needs to be in the boiling water from the USDA's National Center for Home Food Preservation. Follow the timing instructions for the particular food exactly. No rounding up or down, or your food may be prone to spoiling. Blanching times generally range from three to five minutes, but underblanching stimulates the enzymes that cause spoilage and may be worse for the vegetables than no blanching at all. But when you overblanch, the food starts to lose its color, flavor, and nutrients.

**5.** As soon as the produce has completed its blanching time in the boiling water, take it out of the boiling water and plunge it into the ice water to stop the cooking. Leave it in the ice water for the same length of time it was in the boiling water.

**6.** Drain thoroughly. Be sure the produce is completely dry before you freeze or can it.

# HIDDEN STORAGE

APARTMENT DWELLERS AND COLLEGE STUDENTS LIVING IN DORMS KNOW THAT if you can't find space, you make it. No matter what kind of home you live in, you can find places to store food you've preserved yourself.

*Bookshelves.* What's holding your complete Funk & Wagnalls or your collection of original Nancy Drew mysteries in place? A few gleaming jars of canned vegetables or jam would sure look nicer than an old bookend.

*Under your bed.* Lots of people store sweaters or extra bed linens in plastic boxes underneath their beds. Jars fit there, too. If you don't have enough clearance beneath the bed, you can raise it with lifters you get where you shop for bedding and other housewares.

*Closets.* Cool, dark, and dry. Out of the way, but accessible. A shelf at the top of your closet or an unused spot in the back is an ideal place to stash canned or dried food.

*Behind doors.* Closets also have doors, often with plenty of clearance behind them to add a rack that can hold several rows of jars or containers full of dried food.

*Basements and garages.* Conditions in a basement are just about ideal for storing baskets of potatoes, apples, and other produce that keeps without refrigeration. Cover the baskets or boxes with old sheets or burlap to keep pests out. A heated (or at least well-insulated) garage is a handy place to store baskets of food, too, but not if temperatures drop below freezing. Attics are dark and should be dry, but they're rarely cool, so don't store food there.

*Storage lockers.* If you live in an apartment building with storage lockers, make some space there for preserved food. Your locker may be full, but look around to see if others are not using all of their space, and ask if they might consider sharing it with you in exchange for good food.

*Staircases.* The space beneath a flight of stairs diminishes as the steps descend, so that area is rarely used for anything. But it is a good place to look for room to store preserved food. Even if the space is behind dry wall, opening it up and installing a door is a basic job.

# Pickling

## BEST FOR PICKLING

| | |
|---|---|
| Beets | Okra |
| Cabbage | Peppers |
| Cucumbers | Watermelon rind |

**Vinegar is also known as acetic** acid, and as you'll see in many sections of this book, it is helpful in a variety of ways for homesteaders. Right here, I'll explain how you can use it to preserve food.

Pickles are simply food that's preserved in a solution made from vinegar, salt, and spices. Cucumbers are the classic pickled food—and an essential accessory to a well-made hamburger—but lots of other food you grow yourself can be pickled. You can preserve peppers and tomatoes, beets and cabbage, watermelon rinds and okra, even eggs this way.

*These are the quickest and easiest pickles you can make. Start with a "pickling" variety of cucumber—salad varieties have a large seed cavity and a lot of moisture, so they don't stay as crisp. Cut them into spears or coins—your choice.*

*You don't need mason-type canning jars for refrigerator pickles—almost any jar is acceptable. Just be sure they are thoroughly clean. (Run them through the hottest cycle in your dishwasher, or wash them with liquid dish soap and the hottest water you can stand.)*

*You can buy seasoning mix for refrigerator pickles at the grocery store, but if you want to make your own from scratch, here's a simple recipe published by the Missouri extension service.*

*Yields 6 pint-size jars*

1½ cups distilled white vinegar

½ cup fresh dill, packed

2 cups thinly sliced onions

1½ cups granulated sugar

½ teaspoon canning or kosher salt

½ teaspoon mustard seeds

½ teaspoon celery seeds

½ teaspoon ground turmeric

6 cups sliced cucumbers,
  thin to medium-thick slices

**1.** In a large saucepan, bring the vinegar to a simmer as you add other ingredients.

**2.** When the salt and sugar have dissolved and the mix is simmering steadily, pack the cucumbers into clean jars, then pour the hot vinegar mix over them to about a quarter-inch from the top. Some people report that adding a few grape leaves to the bottom of the jar helps the pickles stay crisper. I'm not convinced, but it can't hurt.

**3.** Let the pickles and brine cool on the counter, uncovered, for a couple of hours, until the jars are cool to the touch. Screw the lids on and store them in the refrigerator. Allow them to cure, or soak up the flavor, in the refrigerator for a week, and then they're ready to eat. They'll keep for up to two months refrigerated.

**4.** If you want to keep "fresh-pack" (unfermented) pickles like these outside the refrigerator, you can process and seal the jars in a boiling water or pressure canner. In that case, you need to use standard canning jars to ensure a tight, safe seal (see page 117 for basic water bath canning instructions).

# FERMENTED PICKLES

**The classic, full-flavored sour dills** and bread-and-butter pickles you get at a deli or with a burger are easy to make. All you do is soak cucumbers in a brine solution made with water, salt, vinegar, sugar, and seasonings. As they ferment in the brine, a protective coating of naturally occurring lactic acid forms on the cucumbers' skins, slowly changing them from bright green to olive green and preserving the pickles' crisp texture. To make your own dill pickles with real fresh-from-the-barrel flavor, follow these basic steps.

*Yields 2 gallons*

8 pounds pickling cucumbers
1 cup white wine or cider vinegar
1 cup canning or pickling salt
1 bunch fresh dill
4 to 6 cloves garlic

**1.** Start with firm, warty pickling cucumbers. You can slice them into spears after you wash them well, but the classic pickle from the barrel is whole and you slice it as you eat it.

**2.** In a large saucepan, heat two quarts of water and the vinegar, then gradually add the salt and stir until it has dissolved. Turn off the heat. The kind of salt you use is important. Pickling or canning salt is made without the anticaking ingredient that standard table salt has, which can make your brine cloudy and can alter the color of your pickles. Also, for best results use white wine or cider vinegar that is 5% acetic acid (sometimes labeled as "50 grain").

**3.** You need a container in which to store the pickles while they ferment. Wooden barrels are classic, but if you can't get one or don't have room for one, you can buy a ceramic crock designed for pickling or pick up a food-grade plastic container with a lid (many restaurants and corporate cafeterias discard them every day). You need one gallon of container space for each five pounds of fresh cucumbers, so for this batch be sure to have a container that holds at least two gallons.

**4.** Put the cucumbers in the container. Add a couple handfuls of fresh dill and the garlic to the cucumbers. Pour the brine (salt, water, and vinegar solution) over the cucumbers until they're all covered or floating. The cucumbers need to stay completely submerged in the brine while they are fermenting. Because they float, you need to keep them below the brine's surface. If you're not using a pickling crock that's designed for this, set a plate that's slightly smaller than the container's opening on top of the brine and weigh it down an inch or two with a few cans or rocks. If the container's lid doesn't fit on, drape a large bath towel over it to keep insects and dirt from getting in while the pickles are fermenting.

**5.** Move the container to an out-of-the-way spot where the temperature stays in the mid-sixties to mid-seventies. Temperatures that are too high can cause the cucumbers to spoil before they're cured by the brine.

**6.** As the cucumbers ferment, a thin layer of whitish mold or scum forms on top of the brine. (Yes, I know—yuck.) Check the container a few times a week and skim off the mold. But if the pickles themselves become soft and slimy, or if you catch a whiff of a rotting scent, something has gone wrong and you should dump the cucumbers and start over. Not enough salt in the brine is often the reason the cucumbers start to rot before they're pickled.

**7.** Pickling is a great lesson in patience. You can sample the pickles throughout the process, but they typically reach their best flavor after four to six weeks of fermentation. You'll know the pickles are ready when they snap crisply and when you take a bite you get full flavor all the way to their core. If you're going to eat all of your pickles in about a month, you can eat them right out of the container they fermented in. To keep them longer, you need to pack them in jars with fresh, heated brine, then process and seal the jars in a boiling water or pressure canner.

## OTHER PICKLING VEGETABLES

Sweet and hot peppers, okra, cauliflower, beets, cabbage, onions, zucchini, and watermelon rinds all can be pickled in a similar fermentation process. The first couple times you try to pickle, use tested recipes from the National Center for Home Food Preservation or cookbooks with credibility. To get results that are safe and appetizing, you need to get the brine's acidity and salt levels just right, and they vary for each vegetable.

## RELISH, CHUTNEY, CHOW-CHOW, AND PICCALILLI

You don't have to stop at pickling just one kind of vegetable. Relish, chutney, chow-chow, and piccalilli are condiments made from different mixes of vegetables such as tomatoes (red or green), onions, carrots, corn, beans, and cauliflower. You pickle them all together and then seal them in jars. By the way, they make great gifts for hostesses and other situations where a little homemade something is appropriate.

## HERB VINEGAR

You can't pickle herbs—though dill and other seasonings are critical to making other kinds of pickles—but you can use vinegar to preserve the flavor of rosemary, thyme, sage, tarragon, and other fresh, homegrown herbs. Add spices such as garlic, hot pepper, or grated horseradish to add a little more zip. Or use herbs such as lemon verbena or mint along with berries to make a sweeter topping for fruit or other dishes.

Start with glass jars or bottles that are clear or lightly tinted and that will be easy to fill and pour from. You can recycle used jars and bottles for herb vinegar, but be sure they are completely clean and dry before you begin.

Pick herbs from your garden or buy them. Rinse them to clean off any debris that stuck to the leaves and stems, and then let them dry completely. Gently crush or otherwise slightly bruise the herbs to release their essential oils (the source of their flavors and scents). Push the herbs into the bottles or jars until they are loosely packed to about one-third full.

Use the best-quality vinegar you can afford for this. White wine, red wine, rice wine, and cider vinegars all work for this purpose. Bring the vinegar to a boil, then, using a funnel, carefully pour it into your containers up to a half-inch from the top. Allow the vinegar to cool on the counter to room temperature, and then stopper or put lids on the bottles or jars. Leave them in a cool, dark place to steep for three to four weeks. Shake the bottles or jars from time to time to mix the vinegar and herbs together well.

Herb-infused vinegar is great for salad dressing, as a marinade for grilling meat or vegetables, or in any dish where you want a hint of herb flavor. You can strain out the herbs or leave them in the vinegar. Or put a nice label on it, tie a bow around it, and give it as a gift.

Before we leave this topic, a word about infusing oils (rather than vinegar) with herbs, spices, or garlic. Flavored oils can be very tasty and are as easy to make as herbed vinegars: simply fill clean jars with herbs—as directed for herb vinegar—and fill the jars with oil (skip the heating step). But in contrast to highly acidic vinegar, oil is a ripe host for botulism and other undesirable microbes. So if you make flavored oil, be sure to keep it refrigerated after you make it and use it or throw it away within two weeks.

# Cellaring

## BEST FOR CELLARING

| | |
|---|---|
| Garlic | Onions |
| Green tomatoes | Sweet potatoes |
| Potatoes | Winter squash |

**Before every home had a refrigerator** and supermarkets offered a year-round selection of produce, nearly every house had a root cellar, in which the winter's store of vegetables was kept. The cool, dark conditions were just right in the root cellar to allow certain foods to stay fresh enough to eat during the long, dormant season. In the old houses where I spent time as a kid, the root cellar was always the spookiest spot.

Newer houses don't come with root cellars—many don't even have basements—but you can create the conditions for storing food like this, even if you live in an apartment.

## STORAGE VARIETIES

Many of the crops that are harvested in the fall are the best choices for cellaring (neat how that worked out, isn't it?). Winter squash, which includes acorn, butternut, Hubbard, kabocha, and spaghetti types, is very different from summer squash like zucchini and crookneck squash. The winter types develop a thick, hard skin and have relatively dry flesh, so they keep well for months after harvest. Delicata squash (sometimes sold as Sweet Dumpling) is a type of winter squash with a thinner skin, so they don't keep quite as long. (Pumpkins, you might like to know, are not one unique species of winter squash, but rather are varieties from one of several groups of winter squash.) Harvest winter squash after frost has killed the vines and you can't penetrate the skin with your fingernail. Leave the stems on the fruit.

Onions and potatoes may be very juicy when fresh-picked and even after a "curing" period. The storage types are drier and have thicker skins. For onions, store long-keeper yellow onions such as Copra or Yellow Globe. The milder red, white, and yellow Spanish onions don't keep as long. Russet potatoes and other varieties that have a tough skin and are on the starchy side (as opposed to more waxy red potatoes) hold up best in storage. You'll find that some apple varieties store better than others. Generally, the more tart the apple, the firmer the flesh, and the thicker its skin, the longer it will keep. Jonathan is a classic storage apple. Pears don't last quite as long in storage—they are sweeter than apples, so they rot a little faster—but the same rules of thumb apply for choosing varieties to store.

## CURING YOUR STORES

Whether you plan to store onions, potatoes, sweet potatoes, apples and pears, garlic, or winter squash, they all hold up better if you "cure" them a little before you put them into storage. Curing is nothing more complicated than letting them sit in the fresh air until the juices inside settle. After harvesting these crops, rub off any clumps of dirt still stuck to their skin, but do not wash them. Then set them for a

couple weeks where you can spread them out without touching each other, where air circulates freely, and where they won't be in direct sunlight. A shed, covered patio or balcony, or garage works well for this, but any sheltered, well-ventilated spot indoors or out will serve the purpose. Set potatoes, apples and pears, onions and garlic on a screen or grate of some kind to allow air to flow all around them. That may not be possible for heavier squash—instead, rotate them every couple days so that the side touching the ground changes, allowing it to dry evenly.

## HOW TO STORE

When the produce is thoroughly dry on all sides, they are ready for your "cellar." The ideal conditions for storing these crops are cool temperatures (slightly above freezing to 50°F) and a dark space. Onions and squash fare best where the humidity is very low, while potatoes, apples and pears, and sweet potatoes tolerate slightly more humid conditions. Try to keep apples away from other items. In storage, potatoes gradually emit a gas that fosters ripening. Apples are most vulnerable to this gas, which could cause them to rot as they become overripe. Remember that ventilation is critical for all crops, because airflow keeps mold and other destructive microbes from establishing colonies on your food.

Harvest baskets are the traditional vessel for storing produce in the cellar. You can find them at flea markets and yard sales, or you can buy new ones at farm supply stores. Paper grocery bags also work for storing your crops. Don't use plastic bags, which trap humidity. You can use a hard plastic container, if you first drill many ventilation holes in it. You can keep any of these containers in your pantry, coat closet, insulated garage, an unheated attic, an enclosed porch, or any other room that is dark and dry. Or you can create your own small root cellar with the plans on page 133.

If you have the right conditions, the most common mishap in cellar storage is spoiled food. One bad apple (or onion or potato or...) can spoil the whole bunch by becoming a breeding ground for mold and other fungus. Protect your produce in storage by taking the time first to cull out any item that is bruised, has a soft spot, or is damaged in any way. Eat them—they're still safe for you—but don't store them. For items that are more prone to bruising, such as apples and pears, wrap each up individually in sheets of newspaper. With potatoes, onions, sweet potatoes, and garlic, try to use the items on the bottom of the pile first. They get the least air and are the most susceptible to bruising.

## IN-GARDEN STORAGE

Freezing temperatures outside are not so good for growing food, but for a few vegetables, you can use the weather to help store food in your garden you can eat through the cold months and into next year. You'll find all the details on how to do this in the chapter on growing food (see page 24).

You can store carrots, beets, onions, parsnips, and turnips in a cellar, but if you keep them in your garden you save space for other crops that need to be inside. They all taste a bit sweeter after a frost anyway. The flavor of kale, Brussels sprouts, collards, and leeks improve after a couple of light frosts, too. They won't keep in the garden all winter long where there's consistent snow cover, but they can last well into the fall everywhere and into winter where there's little or no snow.

You can't harvest spinach, arugula, mustard, and Asian greens in winter, but you can plant them in late summer to early fall and eat some of the leaves in the fall. When the weather turns cold, you cover them with mulch and wait until they start growing again as soon as temperatures warm up the next spring. You might think of this as storing the plants over the winter, if not the food from the plants. Similarly, cabbage gives you two seasons of harvest. After you cut off the heads to eat this year, you leave the stumps in the ground and pack mulch around them. The following spring you'll have fist-sized, tender, and sweet little cabbages around the stumps' tops. After you clip them off and eat them, pull the stumps and start the season with new cabbage plants.

# TOMATOES FOR THANKSGIVING

THE SUMMER GARDENING SEASON ENDS—FOR MOST OF US LIVING IN THE TEMPERATE zones of North America—as the days get shorter in early fall. While your tomato plants may stay alive, they are not likely to ripen many of the green fruits that still hang on their vines. At least not outside. You can fry green tomatoes (a classic Southern dish) or make green tomato relish. Or you can store them over the next few months as they gradually ripen. They may not taste as good as sun-ripened tomatoes in summer, but you may have a few ready to eat on Thanksgiving Day.

When the tomatoes appear to have stopped ripening or on a day when a hard frost is predicted at night, pick all the tomatoes remaining on your plants. (If you wait until after the frost, the tomatoes' texture will go from juicy to mealy.) Sort them from lightest to darkest green. Tomatoes become a lighter color—often closer to yellow than true green—just before they ripen. These lighter ones are called "breakers" by pros, and if you put them in a brown paper bag with a banana or avocado, they'll be ripe, sweet, and ready to eat in about three days. (As bananas and avocados ripen, they emit ethylene, a gas that is a naturally ripening catalyst.)

Wrap each of the darker green tomatoes in a single sheet of black-and-white newspaper, and put them in a cardboard box with a lid (the kind copier or printer paper comes in). Keep the box in a cool, dry place.

Check the box each week, first to be sure that none of the tomatoes has been damaged and is leaking—one rotting tomato really does spoil the whole bunch. As the weeks pass, check regularly, and you will see the tomatoes ripening. As soon as one develops the slightest hint of red, take it out of the box and put it near other ripening fruit—and get ready to eat it in a few days. The darkest green tomatoes may not appear to be doing much for weeks, but most will eventually ripen. Be patient and enjoy homegrown tomatoes when there's frost on the windows.

# BASEMENT ROOT CELLAR

EVEN IF YOU LIVE IN A HOUSE WITH A FINISHED BASEMENT, YOU CAN STILL HAVE a root cellar. The following are simple plans for transforming just a corner of your basement into a root cellar, with a minimum of know-how and readily available materials.

*Choose the right spot.* Most crops keep best in relatively high humidity, so choose the dampest spot in your basement. Typically the sump pump is in the dampest corner. You need to build this root cellar next to an exterior wall. You want, if possible, to build on a wall that's below grade (underground), because you want the greatest contact with outside soil temperature you can get. If you need to use a wall that's above grade, be sure it doesn't get too much sun. (Use north-facing or shaded walls.)

*Allow for ventilation.* Without ventilation, stored produce spoils. With this plan, you stimulate ventilation by running two pipes through the outside wall. One will be at the highest point of the wall. Both pipes should be about three inches in diameter. Try to pick a site that allows for this easily, such as one that includes a casement window or the like.

Your ventilation pipes can be made with just about any pipe or ducting. I'm giving directions based on using plastic (PVC) pipes, because they are very durable and easy to cut, and you can readily find valves to fit right into it. Cut a length of pipe to reach through the wall. Cut the end straight. Slide a closed blast gate (valve) onto the pipe until it fits snugly against the end of the pipe and just tight enough to resist slightly. Secure the valve in place with three or four screws.

Cut pieces of pipe for the other vent. This one can go through the wall just about anywhere; just add an elbow and a length of pipe running down the inside so that it ends up about a foot from the floor. Add another blast gate in that pipe.

The purpose of these two vents is to create a siphon. Cool air is denser than warm air and collects in low spots. Anytime the air outside your root cellar is cooler than the air inside, the siphon allows warm air to be drawn out and cool air to flow in. As the temperatures outside fluctuate, you get almost continuous air change while keeping the temperature as low as possible.

Which brings us to the reason for the valves. When the temperature outside drops below freezing, you close one of the valves. This stops the siphoning of air, but you still get some venting while protecting the food from freezing. If the outside temperature falls way below freezing, you need to close both valves until the air outdoors warms up again.

Seal the wall around the pipes with aerosol insulating foam to fill in gaps and cracks. After the foam sets, it holds your pipes securely in place.

*Build the walls.* You could build the walls out of just about anything, but, due to the moist conditions, you should splurge on a handful of 2 x 4s made of cedar or other rot-resistant wood for framing, and some moisture-resistant wall board ("green board" sold for use in shower stalls).

Nail one 2 x 4 to the ceiling, fasten another to the concrete floor with a bead of construction adhesive (the kind in caulking gun tubes), and cut the studs to fit between them.

*Cover the walls.* Put the green board on the inside surfaces first. Once the inside panels are glued and screwed in place, stuff the cavities with fiberglass insulation and cover the outsides. With all of the coverings in place, get out the aerosol foam again and shoot it into all of the cracks—

especially between your new wall and the (likely) ragged edges of the old walls.

A root cellar does not need to be airtight, but the tighter it is, the more control you'll have over the air quality and temperature. Plug as many gaps as you can.

*Add the shelves.* Bear in mind that lower shelves will be cooler and wetter, higher shelves will be warmer and dryer. Arrange and space your shelves to accommodate squash and potatoes on the lower shelves, apples and onions higher up.

*Hang a door.* A ready-made door with frame already measured and cut works fine. Or you can make a simple door from quarter-inch plywood and hang it directly on the studs. One customizing touch worth considering is to make the door in two pieces. This way you can open the top half and grab a couple onions without letting out the coldest, dampest air at the bottom of the root cellar.

*Finishing touch.* Fasten a rod to the handle of each blast gate, and run it through the wall into the basement. This way you can open and close the valves without opening the door and spilling the cold air. It also will allow you to see whether the valves are open or closed without opening the door.

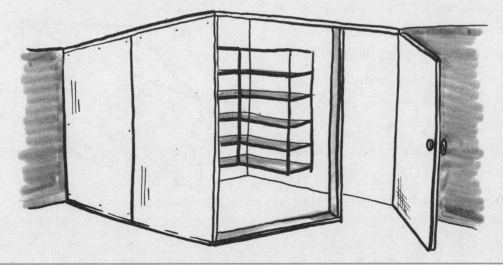

# HOMEMADE CHEESE

CHEESE IS MILK MADE DURABLE AND EASILY PORTABLE. THERE ARE THOUSANDS OF varieties of cheese, and you could apprentice with monks and artisans for decades before you learn all the secrets to making the rich, complex-flavored aged cheeses you find at the gourmet shop. But turning milk into simple fresh cheese is quite easy and quick.

**1.** Pour a gallon of whole milk into a large nonreactive pot. Heat it almost to boiling (190 to 195°F). Stir it constantly to keep the milk scalding as the temperature rises. Remove the pot from the heat and stir in a quarter-cup of white distilled vinegar. Let it stand for ten minutes. As it cools, the milk separates into solids, or curds, and a yellowish liquid called whey.

**2.** Spread a cheesecloth (you see now how it got its name) over a mesh strainer set over the sink. Stir a pinch of salt into the milk, and then pour the entire contents of the pot into the strainer. Leave it draining for an hour.

**3.** Gather up the corners of the cheesecloth and lift it out of the strainer. Roll or pat the curds into a lump ball. You should get about a pound of cheese from a gallon of milk.

**4.** Remove the cheesecloth and wrap the cheese in plastic. Store it in the refrigerator a few hours or overnight to allow it to firm up, and keep it there until you're ready to slice and eat it like you would cream cheese or other soft, spreadable types. It keeps about a week in the refrigerator.

Once you have the most basic steps down, you can get into the nuances that make cheese such an interesting and diverse food. Making cheese requires little work or storage space and no expensive equipment. And you get to be endlessly creative. It's almost ideal home food production for small-space homesteaders.

You start with milk. It can come from a cow, goat, or sheep. It can be pasteurized or "raw"—ultrapasteurized and powdered don't work well. You can go with milk from the store, but if you look around your area, you are certain to discover small dairies where you can get it closer to the source. Cows raised by grazing in a pasture, rather than kept in a stall and given laboratory formulated feed, produce milk that is richer in flavor and full of unique microbes that impact the taste and texture of cheese.

To make cheeses for aging, you need a starter, or a bacteria that acidifies the milk. You can get that from yogurt or cultured buttermilk, or you can buy a bacterial starter from a cheese supply company (you'll find many online). Rennet is a naturally occurring enzyme that converts milk protein from soluble to insoluble. That is, it creates the solid curds from the liquid milk. Rennet is sold in the pudding section of most supermarkets, or you can buy it from a cheesemaking supplier. It comes in tablet or liquid form—most experienced home cheesemakers find the liquid easier to work with and more reliable.

In the basic formula for fresh cheese, the vinegar acidifies the milk, and the natural rennet in the milk forms the curds. More complex cheeses require starter and rennet selected to produce specific reactions. To make hard cheeses, which keep much longer, you need a cheese press, which squeezes moisture out of the curds and compresses them. You can buy or make one. If you have a place in your home where you can manage the temperature and humidity closely, you can make any kind of cheese, from chèvre to bleu, cheddar to Brie.

# HOMEMADE YOGURT

MANY COMMERCIAL BRANDS OF YOGURT ARE MORE LIKE PROCESSED PUDDING than the healthful dairy food full of beneficial cultures that you get when you make it yourself. Turning fresh milk into homemade yogurt is easy and takes ordinary kitchen skills and no special equipment.

Yogurt is made through the action of cultures that you need to add. You can buy it freeze-dried or just use three tablespoons of plain yogurt with live active cultures from the store as the starter for your first batch. After that, you'll have created your own starter to use for future batches. An ordinary heating pad—like you use for sore necks and backs—and an instant-read thermometer will help you keep the milk at exactly the right temperature for the cultures to work efficiently.

1. Start with a half-gallon of milk, which will yield the same amount of yogurt. You can use whole, low-fat or fat-free milk: your preference. Allow the milk and your starter to come to room temperature.

2. Stirring steadily, heat the milk over medium heat to just 185°F, keeping tabs on the temperature with an instant-read thermometer. You can do that in a double-boiler—a smaller pot with the milk heated over boiling water in a larger pot—or you can heat the milk directly on your stove if you do it slowly. Heating the milk kills any microbes that might interfere with the cultures that digest lactose and make yogurt. You'll know you've reached the right temperature because the milk starts to froth but has not yet bubbled. While you're waiting for the milk to heat, fill your sink with ice-cold water to come nearly to the top of the pot.

3. As soon as the milk is warm, remove the pot from the heat and immerse in the cold water, being careful not to get any water in the milk. Stir the milk continuously and cool to 110°F.

4. When the milk reaches 110°F, remove it

from the cold water and stir in the starter or plain yogurt. Mix it thoroughly. At that temperature, the active cultures get busy reproducing and consuming lactose acid. Cover the pot with its lid, turn on the heating pad, and set it for 110°F or its medium level of warmth. Put the pot on the heating pad and cover it with a thick towel.

**5.** Leave the pot alone on the heating pad for seven hours. No stirring, no checking on it, no peeking. Be sure your heating pad doesn't have a safety mechanism to turn itself off after a certain length of time; if that's the case, you'll need to monitor the pad to keep it on.

**6.** When the time is up, lift the lid and look to see that the milk has separated into chunky curds and a little thin liquid on top (whey). It will smell a bit like cheese and the liquid may look greenish: that's what you want. The yogurt will be runnier than store-bought yogurt at this stage, but if it is still mostly liquid, let it sit on the heating pad a little longer next time.

**7.** Give the yogurt a thorough stirring, then pour it into scrupulously clean plastic containers with lids (used yogurt or cottage cheese containers serve well). Put them in the refrigerator to chill overnight and in the morning stir well again. Now you've got homemade yogurt for breakfast. Your homemade yogurt will keep in the refrigerator for about two weeks. Before you finish it, remember to save three tablespoons of it to use as starter for the next batch.

# CHAPTER FOUR:

# WORKING WITH ANIMALS

**D**omesticated animals are more than just a cool addition to your small homestead. They contribute valuable resources to your goal of self-sufficiency, help dispose of waste, and are a source of food themselves. Caring for livestock is a great way to teach kids responsibility. And small animals are genuinely entertaining and fun to have around.

You can raise some kind of livestock no matter where you live. You need no more room than you do for a small garden plot, and you can start with animals that are quiet and discreet enough that your neighbors may never know you have them. Many municipalities today are dropping or loosening restrictions on keeping domesticated animals, even in areas densely populated by people. Before you bring any livestock home, though, be sure to check with your local zoning commission or cooperative extension office about any ordinances that govern keeping domesticated animals at residential (as opposed to agricultural) properties.

# Bees

**From suburban backyards to city** rooftops, bees might be more popular now than Chihuahuas. In a space about the size of a small filing cabinet, you can keep a hive where a healthy colony of bees will live and make honey and come home to when they're done with their important work of pollinating your garden and others. Bees are entertaining to watch, too, as they keep as busy (as the saying goes) building, feeding, and caring for their queen.

I realize many people worry about the dangers of keeping bees, especially around children. But if you don't have an uncontrollable phobia (known as "apiphobia") and no one in your family is highly allergic to bee stings, you needn't be afraid of bees. Unlike wasps, such as the all-too-familiar, bee-resembling yellow jacket, bees typically die when their barbed stinger catches in your skin (it's ripped out of the bees' abdomen, in case you're wondering). So bees sting only in desperation, most commonly to protect the queen. You leave them alone, they'll keep clear of you—though keep in mind that they may be attracted to some kinds of soap, perfume, or other manufactured fragrances. If you'd like to keep bees around but want to be extra-safe, I'll tell you about a truly docile type in the "Choosing breeds" section on the next page.

If you need one more reason not to use pesticides in your garden, remember that many of those chemicals are toxic to bees. Even if you don't keep bees, pesticides are harmful to the many native bees you depend on for pollination.

## BENEFITS

Honey straight from the source is a naturally pure sweetener you can gather and store for yourself. But the most important contribution bees make to your food supply comes from the pollinating they do in your garden. Crops such as cucumbers, peppers, apples, and raspberries—and countless others—rely on bees to spread the pollen from plant to plant. The more pollination that takes place, the bigger your harvest will be. Bees also produce wax, which you can use to make candles, lip balm, and other useful products. With a little more effort, you can harvest royal jelly and propolis, which bees make and are purported to help keep you healthy. Propolis also is used to make wood varnish.

## CHOOSING BREEDS

There are thousands of species of bees, and not all of them produce harvestable honey or even live in a hive. Many common wild bees nest, feed, and care for their larvae in small groups or even alone. Honeybees come from one of four strains that have been domesticated for centuries. The strains are Italian (a.k.a.Western), Caucasian (which refers to the mountains of Eastern Europe, not their skin color), Black, and Grey (or Carniolan). Among them, Italian and Grey bees are the most popular for beekeepers. Grey bees are widely recommended for novice apiarists—that's the technical term for beekeepers—because they are gentle, have strong homing instincts (especially valuable in bustling urban areas), and resist the

viruses and pests that plague other types. They do not, however, fare well in very hot climates, so if you live in the Southeast or Southwest, go with Italian honeybees.

If you want to encourage bees to help with pollinating your garden but are fearful that you or a family member will be stung, you want to attract mason bees. They do not make honey, but they are very docile around people and are easy to attract with a simple structure you can build just by drilling holes in a block of wood. (See page 149 for specifics.)

## FEEDING

Bees live on the carbohydrates they get from nectar (and the honey they make from it) and protein they get from pollen. The best way for you to nourish the bees is to plant a diverse garden full of different herbs, vegetables, and fruits, as well as flowering plants, shrubs, and trees. Your goal is to have some plant or another in bloom from spring through fall, so the bees have a steady nectar supply. A few particular favorites are borage (known as "bee's bread"), lilacs, monarda, and goldenrod. Some beekeepers feed their bees syrup (a simple sugar-and-water solution) in early spring and late fall, when there's little other food for them, and even supplement their diet during the growing season. This is sensible if you live where winters are long and frigid, or where there aren't flowers for them to feed on during the other seasons.

Bees also need water nearby, especially during dry spells. A birdbath or other small, shallow dish of water works well. If you don't keep the water supply constant, the bees may frequent your neighbors' swimming pool or dripping water spigot and cause them to worry about your hive.

## SHELTER

In the wild, honeybees live in hives they construct themselves, most commonly in a hollow section of a tree or in an opening they find in a wall or other manmade structure. They tend to seek out locations that are sheltered in some way from the wind. The hive itself is a series of layers of honeycomb, an amazing example of insect engineering. Honeycomb is made from evenly shaped six-sided "cells" joined together to form a panel. Made of beeswax, the cells are used for storing food (honey) or as a larvae nursery. In the first year of a hive, bees devote much of their time and energy to building honeycomb and less to making honey.

As a beekeeper, you provide the hive for your colony, but your goal is to mimic nature as much as possible. Put it close to a wall, fence, or hedgerow to protect it from the wind and harsh weather. A partially shaded location is the bees' preference. Set the hive as high as you can reach, and the bees coming and going from the hive will mostly fly over the heads of your neighbors. Speaking of, do all you can to place your hive where it won't be seen by passersby— at the least, set the hives twenty-five feet or more from sidewalks and roads.

The most common bee housing used today are called "Langstroth hives," named for a beekeeper in Philadelphia who came up with the design in 1851. It is a box composed of a series of eight to ten wooden or plastic frames in which the bees build their honeycomb. The frames rest on a foundation, usually made of wire, and they are inside a covered box to protect the comb from the elements. This design works for beekeepers because it allows the frames to be removed as they fill up with honey and the honey can be extracted without cutting into the comb.

Today, you may find other backyard beehive designs, notably the top-bar hive, which has honeycomb frames placed horizontally and no foundation. Top-bar hives reportedly produce less honey, but they are closer to how bees build in nature and they're relatively easy to build with salvaged materials.

If you want to go totally "old school," wicker bee "skeps" are the classic and most attractive backyard hive. They're woven from straw into a basket that's rounded on top and open on the bottom. Bee skeps need to be kept on grass or other natural surface—so they don't work well on balconies and rooftops—and they're not likely to produce the most honey or even beeswax, but they give your garden a very authentic look. You can buy a bee skep or take a course in how to make one.

If you're just starting out with beekeeping, your best bet is to buy the Langstroth design hives, because you will find the most information and support from the many others who are using the box hives.

## CARE AND MAINTENANCE

The queen, her workers (females who provide food for the queen and the brood, and care for the hive), and the drones (males whose only purpose is reproduction) have evolved specific roles that help the hive sustain itself. Your role, then, is to stay out of the way and help only when problems occur. By providing the bees with the conditions that they need, you minimize the potential problems. One common mistake that many new beekeepers make is setting up a hive that is too big for the size of the colony. The extra space leaves room that the bees can't police themselves, creating an opportunity for pests that prey on bees to move in.

Wax moths, beetles, mites and viruses sometimes invade honeybee hives, and there are a variety of chemical treatments available for dealing with them. Many beekeepers, though, are able to do without the pesticides and antibiotics, relying instead on the bees' natural defenses to overcome problems. For instance, wax moths often get into a hive (attracted by the wax, hence their name) and lay eggs. When the larvae (little grubs) hatch, they eat honeycomb and honey, spin webbing into a cocoon, and turn into moths. In a healthy colony the bees kill the grubs before they do much damage.

If you are keeping bees to harvest their honey, you want to have a protective suit that looks sort of like a cross between the protective gear you wear when handling hazardous materials and the outfits worn by spacemen in comic books. You also want a "bee smoker," a small vessel in which you burn bark, pine needles, dried grass or sage, paper, or other light fuel and then puff it into the hive with the smoker's bellows. Smoke causes the bees to gorge on honey, and they become more docile, so you can open up the hive without exciting them too much. The best times to go into your hives are when temperatures are below 90 degrees, when nearby flowers are in full bloom and the nectar is abundant, and during the midday hours when the workers are out in the field collecting nectar. Early to mid-summer is typically the best time for people to gather honey.

Experienced beekeepers use a specially designed extractor to separate honey from the comb. Find a local beekeepers' association, and offer to help another beekeeper with the process, then you may be able to borrow an extractor when you are ready to harvest your own. The simple, low-tech way is just to crush the comb with the honey inside in a bucket that has a screen to catch the comb and a spigot at the bottom called a "honey gate," from which it drips out. You can find buckets with this design where beekeeping supplies are sold.

## HABITS

A normal honeybee colony has between 20,000 and 50,000 members, with one queen. When the hive becomes crowded (or if the current queen is more than two years old), they may crown a second queen, and half of the members swarm out of the hive with the new queen to scout out a location for a new hive. A swarm may alarm your neighbors, as it can appear to be a gang of unruly stingers preparing to attack, even if that's not generally the case. The best way to prevent swarming is to introduce a new queen to your hive every spring. If you do find a swarm of bees you or others are worried about, you can hire a "swarm catcher" who captures the bees and gives (or sells) them to other beekeepers. Again, getting involved with a local beekeepers' association can help you find the resources you need when situations like these arise.

Unlike many types of bees, honeybees survive through the winter. They are not active, but instead cluster together for warmth. Some researchers have found the temperature of a cluster of bees inside their hive to be about 93°F, even when it's below freezing outside.

## GETTING STARTED

Early spring is the time for you to start your beehive. You can order bees from a mail-order source, which will send you a package with a queen and several thousand workers. You may be able to get a colony from a swarm catcher in your area, but I suggest you start with a beginner's kit, if you've never kept bees before. Be sure to have your hive and all your supplies ready to go before you order. When the bees do arrive, late afternoon on an overcast day is the best time to introduce them to your new hive.

The Resources section on page 253 will guide you to reputable suppliers of bees and beekeeping gear, as well as how to find a beekeepers' group near you.

## HONEY DO

WHETHER YOU HARVEST YOUR OWN HONEY OR BUY IT FROM A LOCAL BEEKEEPER, it is a valuable local resource. Here are a few fascinating facts about it.

- Honey stays fresh at room temperature. No need to refrigerate it.
- Cookies, cakes, and other baked goods made with honey stay fresher longer because honey absorbs and retains moisture.
- Honey has natural antiseptic properties and has been used for centuries to coat open wounds and protect them from infection.
- Your grandmother was right: Tea with honey soothes a sore throat. That's because honey reduces inflammation.

# MASON BEE HOUSE

**Small Space Project**

MASON BEES, ALSO SOMETIMES CALLED "ORCHARD BEES" OR *OSMIA LIGNARIA*, are very people-friendly pollinators found throughout North America. They tend to be slightly smaller than a honeybee, and their bodies are shiny dark blue. Mason bees don't produce honey, but they are active at pollinating fruit trees as well as vegetable plants early in the growing season. They don't live in a hive—they nest in existing holes in wood. For that reason, the tube design of this mason bee house is sure to attract them to your yard.

**1.** At the home center or lumberyard, get posts cut from a hardwood such as fir or redwood. You may also be able to find an old fence post that will work for this, but don't use pressure-treated wood. You'll end up with blocks four to six inches wide and six inches deep: each block will make one bee house. They can be from one to two feet long.

**2.** With a 5/16 bit, drill rows of holes, each about 3/4-inch apart, from one end of the block to the other (*figure A*). Drill the holes all the way through the block. A drill press, if you have access to one, makes this so much easier than a hand drill. Maybe you can find one to use at a local trade school or business.

**3.** Nesting females are attracted to dark sur-

faces. Use a blowtorch to lightly char the side where you started the holes (*figure B*).

**4.** Waterproof the blocks by dipping them once in water-based polyurethane (*figure C*). Be sure to let any excess sealant drain away. Leave the blocks to dry for several days.

**5.** Seal the back of the house (the uncharred side) with tape (*figure D*). Duct or even painter's tape will work. More expensive foil tape looks better. Be sure the tape is sealed tight all around the edges of the block.

**6.** Get paper straws or tubes—the thinner the walls the better—that fit snugly in the holes. Paper straw inserts make it easy to clean out old nests each season and help control mites that parasitize the bees. Use black pen or nail polish to darken the straws' tips—again, the dark color is more appealing to nesting females (*figure E*).

**7.** Cut the straws (not the black end) to be slightly shorter than the hole, and slide them in (*figure F*). The ends should just touch the tape covering the back of the holes: this will make it a cinch to remove the tape and clean or replace the straws each year.

**8.** Sprinkle fine sand over the face of the block, letting it fall through the holes, to cover the sticky tape at the back of the holes and to help wedge the straws in place.

**9.** Twirl a pencil in the tip of each straw to set the straw and clear its entrance (*figure G*).

**10.** Cut a small piece of plywood slightly larger than the wood block and nail it on top to create an overhang, like a roof, that shelters the entrance to the holes (*figure H*).

**11.** Bees naturally nest in a spot that gets morning sun and is protected from the wind. Hang your bee house under the eave on the southeast side of your house, or on a shed, fence post, or some solid structure. Be sure it is at least three feet off the ground. Nail it in place.

**12.** Each November, when the bees' active season is over, remove the straws. Clean them out thoroughly with a vinegar and water solution, or just replace them.

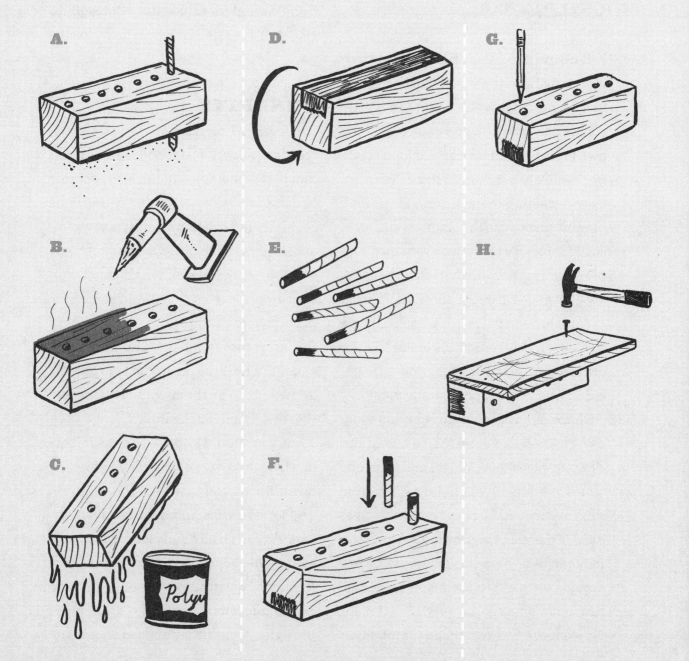

**A.**

**B.**

**C.**

**D.**

**E.**

**F.**

**G.**

**H.**

# Chickens

**I'm convinced that plants can pro-**vide us with all the nutrients we need to live a long, healthy life, so there's no reason we couldn't grow and gather all of our own food. But animal-derived foods taste good and are very satisfying, so many of us enjoy eating them. Caring for a small flock of chickens is the simplest and most sustainable way to produce your own supply of animal protein. A healthy hen lays an egg at least every three days from spring through fall. With a flock of just a half dozen chickens and a small lawn or other open outdoor area, you can get enough eggs to supply a family of four.

Chickens do need a little attention every day, but really no more than a dog or cat. The setup cost isn't much, and it can be almost nothing if you build a coop from salvaged materials. They feed themselves most of the year (the growing season), and they can be a help with your garden. They develop distinct, often amusing personalities, and some can be very affectionate. No wonder city-dwellers and suburbanites from Brooklyn to Seattle, Chicago to Houston, are raising their own flocks like never before.

## BENEFITS

For decades Americans, especially homesteaders, depended on eggs as an important part of their diet. In the 1970s doctors began advising patients that eating eggs regularly led to an unhealthy amount of cholesterol in the blood, a cause of heart disease, stroke, and other ailments. Egg consumption went down, and some people turned to eating only egg whites. Now the latest research has found that whole eggs are a healthful source of lean protein, and we can eat them without worrying that they'll ruin our health.

But you should know that eggs freshly laid by hens that spend their days grazing outside are different from eggs produced on factory farms and sold in supermarkets. As you've no doubt seen in the news, salmonella outbreaks are an all-too-frequent occurrence among factory-raised chickens because they are living in unhealthy conditions and fed an unnatural diet. (To keep chickens from cannibalizing each other, which they are prone to do in the very confined spaces of factories, they are often debeaked!) Eggs laid by hens that graze for their own food have been found in many studies to be richer in vitamins A and E, and in essential omega-3 fatty acids, and are lower in cholesterol, too. By raising your own chickens, you get eggs that are healthier for you and your family, and you stop supporting the inhumane—and often dangerous—factory production of eggs.

The ideal diet for healthy chickens is based on bugs and seeds they scrounge up for themselves, but it can also include vegetable scraps from your kitchen and garden, and even weeds. Chickens are even more efficient than a compost pile at turning waste into nutrients for your garden plants. In fact, chicken manure is very rich in nitrogen and can dramatically heat up your compost pile, making the best and most natural fertilizer possible. Even better, if you keep them in a moveable coop (often called a "chicken tractor"), their scratching, eating, and pooping can transform almost any plot of ground into a highly fertile garden plot.

Healthy chickens may live up to twenty years, though the average is eight to ten years. Their egg production declines during the second half of their lives, but they're so much fun, it's easy to become attached to them as pets. You can decide when, if ever, each becomes more appealing to you as meat.

## CHOOSING BREEDS

Hens of all breeds lay eggs, but the different breeds are categorized depending on whether they produce a lot of eggs (layers) or are better suited for meat production (broilers, fryers, or roasters), though some are defined as "dual purpose." If a steady supply of eggs is your goal, go with layers.

Bantam chickens are about half the size of standard breeds. Bantams' eggs are a bit smaller than the standards, too. But aside from those differences, you'll find that the petite hens have the same wide variety of traits—of plumage and personality—as you see in the standard breeds. If you have less than a quarter-acre to graze them on, go with bantams; otherwise, choose whichever size you prefer.

You can choose from more than 400 different breeds of chickens. For your first time, consider trying a few different ones to see which best suit your purposes and conditions. For instance, some breeds tolerate sweltering summers or frigid winters better than others. Certain breeds are more dominant or submissive, aggressive or docile. Productivity and longevity vary from breed to breed, too. Some hens make better and more meat than others. And, of course, there is appearance. The feather patterns on hens can be as fanciful as a high-fashion model or as traditional as a farm wife. Egg colors vary, too, from white and brown to blue, green, and speckled. Color does not reflect the eggs' nutritional value, as you may have heard, but the variety of hues does make your egg collection basket more interesting. Finally, just like with vegetables, these days you can choose an heirloom breed of chickens that's been around for centuries or a recent hybrid with unique traits that are valuable to you.

A few breeds that are popular for smaller flocks include Buff Orpington, Barred Plymouth Rock, Araucana, and Wynadottes. Start small—six to eight hens—in your first season to be sure you have the time and space to manage a flock. As with a garden, it's easier to grow your commitment than to go big to begin with and have to scale back when your effort gets beyond your control.

## FEEDING

Insects and seeds they find for themselves on the ground are the solid foundation of a healthy diet for chickens. They also eat small weeds (particularly the aptly named chickweed) and, if you let them, seedlings in your garden, too. And, as I previously mentioned, chickens feed on kitchen and garden scraps, especially leafy greens. Don't give them meat or dairy products. Some people report that giving chickens onions and garlic affects the flavor of their eggs, and that feeding them citrus fruits or their rinds diminishes egg production. Best to avoid those.

During the cold months and at other

times when your chickens are not able to scrounge up their own food, you can give them store-bought pellets, typically comprising cracked corn for carbohydrates and soybean meal for protein. In feed stores and online, you'll find mixes that are formulated for new chicks, for broilers, for breeding, and for layers. The right feed for your hens keeps them healthy and productive, but beware of products that have preventive medications and other chemicals in them—your small flock with access to the outdoors will be naturally healthy. Go with certified organic feed, and you can be sure it's pure.

A feeding trough designed for chickens minimizes waste. You can often find a used one at a barn sale or online. But a feeder isn't necessary—for a small flock you can use a few small plates.

Chickens need a constant supply of fresh water. You can buy water containers plain or fancy for your chickens—again barn sales are a good place to search for one. Or you can make a very simple one with a large metal can (the number 10 size that cafeteria and restaurant supplies come in is best) and an eight-inch metal pie plate. Be sure both are thoroughly clean before you start. About an inch from the open end of the can, drill or punch two small (quarter-inch or so) holes on opposite sides. Fill the can with water, then place the plate, bottom side up, over the open end. Flip it over and the plate will replenish itself as the chickens drink the water. Just be sure to keep the can consistently filled—chickens drink a lot on cool and hot days.

Grit is tiny, tiny pebbles stored in chickens' crops (or gizzards) that take the place of teeth, helping them to digest their food. Chickens that graze find their own grit, but you have to supply it if your hens are confined. Likewise, calcium is critical to making strong eggshells. You can provide it in the form of crushed oyster shells, sold both in feed stores and in garden centers.

## SHELTER

Setting up a proper home for your little flock is critical to their health, safety, and productivity, but it's also a fun chance for you to get creative with the design and materials. The first choice you have to make is whether you want the coop to be stationary or mobile. A henhouse that stays put is simpler and may be all you have room for. But if you can and want to graze your chickens in different spots around your property—to get them to stir up and fertilize garden beds or to give them a constant supply of fresh plants and bugs to eat—you can keep the flock in a chicken tractor, a coop that's easily moved to different spots.

You can buy prebuilt chickens coops of either type, and online you can find lots of photos and plans to make your own, too. Homesteaders are using all kinds of pre-existing structures to make coops and chicken runs, from toolsheds and garages to doghouses and plastic outdoor storage containers. The simplest ones are wood A-frames wrapped in chicken wire and with a small house at one end.

No matter which type you choose to go with, the basics of an effective coop are the same. Chickens need shelter from extreme cold and heat and protection from predators including hawks, foxes, dogs, cats, and raccoons. (Wildlife like foxes, raccoons, and hawks are increasingly common in cities today.) Almost any structure with a sturdy roof and walls works. A healthy home gives each hen four to five square feet of inside space.

Chickens prefer to sleep perched above ground level. Put a ladder, chair, tree branches, or shelf in your coop—or anything they can stand on that's higher than the floor—and they will roost on it. Nesting boxes, filled with straw, shredded paper, or other soft, natural material, encourage the hens to lay their eggs where you can find them. You don't, by the way, need one nest for each bird—they readily share even when there are open nests.

The healthiest place for your chicken coop is over bare ground, where the droppings can be naturally decomposed by worms and other creatures in the soil. Keeping a constant layer of leaves, dried grass, straw, wood shavings, or shredded newspaper (all carbon-rich materials, as we'll cover in the section on composting on page 178) helps the high nitrogen bird poop to decompose quickly and with less odor. If you must keep your chickens on a concrete or other solid floor, install a wire mesh base to your coop to make cleanup easier (the droppings fall through to the floor where you can more easily sweep them up). Spread a layer of the carbon-rich stuff underneath the wire mesh. Either way, every other week or so, clean out the bedding and waste, dump it in your compost pile (which will heat up in hours!), and replace it with fresh bedding material.

For extra protection from daylight predators such as dogs and hawks, some homesteaders are using electric mesh fencing, which the chickens quickly learn to avoid. It is relatively inexpensive and very effective, so you can leave your flock to graze in safety. But, having never used it, I still think a movable coop with ordinary chicken wire that's slightly larger than a standard raised garden bed (four feet by ten feet) seems more appropriate for a homestead-size flock.

## HABITS

A healthy, well-cared-for hen lays an egg every other day or so (some breeds more, some less) from early spring into fall. During winter, when the daylight hours are shorter, egg production naturally slows down and the chickens molt, shedding most of their feathers and growing a new set. They will keep laying through most of this period if a small light is left on for a few hours each morning (it works best if the light is consistent, like on a timer). Some experts believe, though, that this practice causes the chicken to stop laying at a younger age. By the way, feathers that have been shed make a healthy addition to your compost pile.

Chickens roll around in dirt to help them get rid of mites and parasites that get into their feathers. If your chickens don't have a place where they can dig their own dirt baths, give them one in a box. Just fill a shallow box with equal parts coarse sand, wood ashes, soil, and diatomaceous earth, a naturally occurring mineral that works as an organic pest control (just be sure to get it from a garden supplier, not the kind used in swimming pool filters). If you want to be entertained, watch your hens take a bath on a hot, dry day, flopping around front and back, side to side, stirring up a cloud of dust.

## GETTING STARTED

Early spring is the ideal time to launch your own flock of chickens. I can't answer the philosophical question about which came first, the chicken or the egg, but I can tell you that the easiest way to begin a backyard flock is to buy pullets. They are hens that are four to five months old, just the age when they start laying eggs. Pullets cost more than baby chicks, they're not nearly as adorable, and your breed choices might be limited, but pullets are ready to go right into the coop. If you do decide to start with baby chicks, be prepared to keep them in a warm place that's fully protected from predators—most chicken owners let them live inside the house during this period—and to check on them several times a day for the first month or two. They also need a lamp for heat (a 250-watt bulb is ideal).

If at all possible, get female chickens only. Hens lay eggs whether a rooster is present or not. Roosters may protect the flock from some predators, but they also make a lot of noise—all day long, not just at sunrise—which can disturb your neighbors and cause them to complain about your chickens.

You can mail-order for pullets and chicks (I've listed a couple of popular sources in the "Resources" chapter, page 253), but buying from a nearby hatchery saves you money on shipping, is less disruptive for the birds, and supports local farms (which slows suburban sprawl). However, you may not find a lot different breeds to choose from in your area and with the growing popularity of backyard chickens, the supplies tend to go fast in spring. Wherever you get your pullets or chicks, get about 20% more of them than you want to compensate for any losses (and yes, losses are not uncommon) you suffer on their way to full adulthood.

Once your hens are ready to be outside in the coop, keep them confined to it for about five days to establish that it is their permanent home. Then they always will return to it at night, because, as the old saying goes, chickens do come home to roost.

## EGG-CELLENT EGGS

FRESHLY LAID EGGS ARE MORE FLAVORFUL AND NUTRITIOUS THAN THOSE THAT have been pasteurized and shipped to supermarkets, where they stay for several weeks. To get the most from the fresh eggs your own hens lay or that you get from a local farmer, remember these facts:

- Fresh eggs keep for several days without refrigeration. For maximum freshness, store them with the pointy (narrower) side down.

- You may notice traces of dirt or chicken droppings on fresh eggs. Before you scrub them clean, bear in mind that the outside of the shell has a thin membrane, called "the bloom" that protects it from undesirable bacteria and other microbes. If you can't easily rub off the dirt with your fingers, wipe it gently with a towel dipped in a solution of half warm water and half white vinegar.

- Be sure to wash your hands thoroughly before and after handling the eggs.

# Mixed Poultry

**Guinea fowl, ducks, and geese are** not as popular as chickens are among modern homesteaders, but many people who have lots of experience with them believe that mixing a few different kinds of poultry is ideal for small backyard flocks. They all feed on bugs and leave behind manure to fertilize your garden. Like chickens, they lay eggs you can gather and eat. They're all easy to care for even in relatively small spaces and tend to be even more self-sufficient than chickens. And because each type of bird has its own niche, they will live companionably on your homestead.

## BENEFITS

If you think chickens are reliable egg producers, certain breeds of ducks are known to lay more than 300 eggs a year; like chickens, egg-laying slows down in winter when the ducks molt. Duck eggs average about the size of the jumbo chicken eggs you see in the supermarket. (Keep in mind, though, that egg sizes vary among chickens, ducks, and other poultry, but you never see that in the store because they are sorted by size in the processing plant before they are packed and shipped.) Fresh eggs from ducks allowed to graze taste very similar to fresh, free-range chicken eggs, with the same orange-tinted yolks and firm whites. Duck eggs have a slightly "ducky" flavor much as fresh chicken eggs taste a bit like cooked chicken breast. Guinea fowl lay eggs that are a half to three-quarters the size of large chicken eggs, but they are not as inclined to use the nest so you have to hunt for them. The egg-laying period for geese is shorter, generally from late spring to early fall, and the eggs are higher in fat and protein than chicken and duck eggs. Some bakers prefer using eggs from ducks or geese because the whites (technically, albumen) stay stiffer and makes cakes and cookies more airy.

Guineas are voracious consumers of ticks, which makes them appealing to anyone whose home is near woodlands and other breeding grounds for the nasty little pests, and they love beetles, too.

They are not scratchers or plant-eaters, like chickens, so they stroll through gardens eating bugs and leave crops alone. Ducks eat a wide variety of insects, with a particular taste for slugs, the bane of wet-climate gardeners. They may also eat grass, weeds, and other plants. Geese are strictly vegetarian, and they have been used for centuries to clear gardens and other cultivated lands of weeds. They'll virtually mow your lawn for you.

All types of domesticated fowl produce a substantial amount of nitrogen-rich manure that heats up a compost pile in a hurry, which is especially valuable if you add a lot of carbon-heavy materials like leaves or paper. The resulting compost will be the best fertilizer money can't buy.

## CHOOSING BREEDS

Among the many types of guineas, the most popular for backyard flocks are Helmeted Guineafowl (*Numida meleagris*). Their feathers are black and gray with white dots, and they grow to be about four pounds. This species is very social and attentive to hatching its eggs.

If you want lots of duck eggs, Khaki Campbell ducks are champion producers—as many as 300-plus eggs a year each. They are taupe-colored with green beaks and good foragers. Muscovy ducks are even better at foraging, but they are (to most people's taste) not very attractive and they're distinctly not very friendly to people or other creatures. Indian Runners and Pekins are well-adapted to mixed flocks and they look like ducks from storybooks—cream- to yellow-colored feathers with orange beaks and feet. Pekins grow a bit larger, reaching as big as nine pounds, while an average Indian Runner is closer to four pounds. In Europe, where people eat more duck than in North America, Rouens are the most popular duck for meat. They look like Mallards, the ducks you see most often at your local pond.

You won't find many different breeds of geese to choose from, but the most widely available is the Toulouse. It is very cold-hardy, lays about fifty eggs a year and can grow as large as twenty-five pounds. It is gray on the back and breast, white underneath. Pilgrims are known to be very friendly and quieter than other breeds. The males are white, the females olive-gray. They grow to be about fifteen pounds. Embden are the classic-looking goose with white feathers and orange beaks and legs.

## FEEDING

Backyard poultry allowed to roam and feed to their hearts' content mostly fill themselves up with the natural foods they prefer—bugs, seeds, and small plants. You can supplement their grazing with fruit and vegetable waste from your kitchen or nearby restaurants. The birds often go for wilted lettuce greens, carrot tops, broccoli stalks, apple cores, and the like—experiment to see which your birds prefer. You can also give them a small amount of whole grain, such as corn, oats, or wheat.

During winter and other times when their natural food is scarce, you can buy pelleted food formulated specifically for each type of fowl. They can all survive on chicken feed, if that's all you can find, but stay away from the medicated products, which are not necessary for these free-range birds and may actually harm them. Also, keep in mind that when the temperatures are low, birds eat more so that their metabolism can help them stay warm. You can feed them from small dog bowls or any other stable, easy-to-access dish.

Your poultry flock needs a constant supply of drinking water. Of course, ducks and geese prefer to get it while they're wading, but when any of them can't find it outside, you need to be sure they have access to a fresh supply. You can buy or make a self-replenishing container—either way, for ducks and geese it needs to be deeper to accommodate their bills than the water supply needs to be for chickens and guineas.

## SHELTER

The basic housing requirements for ducks, geese, and guineas are even simpler than they are for chickens. They need shelter from extreme temperatures and harsh weather (high winds, heavy rain, or snow), and they need protection from most of the same predators that threaten chickens. You can house guineas and chickens together, if you have both.

Almost any sort of enclosure works—my neighbor uses a small doghouse and a chain-link dog pen for her ducks. You can build a more elaborate structure—Duckingham Palace, as one renowned gardener calls his—but that is more for aesthetics than any need your fowl have.

Guineas prefer to roost in trees rather than indoors; ducks and geese do not roost. All three are more inclined to create their own nests rather than lay eggs in boxes you provide. In fact, guineas tend to hide their nests so you may never see them unless you keep a watchful eye on them. For that reason and because the eggs are about half the weight of a chicken's, many guinea owners don't bother with trying to gather the eggs. A duck or goose lays its eggs in the same place each day, though the spot is mostly of its own choosing.

Many people who keep ducks and geese provide them with a small plastic kiddie pool, if they don't have access to a pond. Protect them from parasites and other problems by changing the water every two or three days. The bird droppings in the water are valuable nutrients for your garden plants, so if at all possible pour it off into the soil—not directly on plants, though, because the "hot" nitrogen can burn the leaves.

To protect their ducks from daytime predators (like dogs and cats) and to protect gardens from ducks, some homesteaders keep them in a portable pen, like a chicken tractor. They come back to their pen on their own at night, so the portable pen isn't essential for them.

## HABITS

Guineas can be noisy, screeching at intruders and other creatures that frighten them. They make good "watchdogs" for this reason, but the noise may disturb the neighbors. They also like to roost on deck railings and other perches. Since they don't know property lines, they may surprise your neighbors by showing up on their side of the line. Before you get guineas, it's a smart idea to inform your neighbors and get their acceptance. Be sure to tell the neighbors that guineas eat pests, mice as well as insects, and they do become accustomed to familiar people and pets.

Ducks are much quieter and docile. They naturally walk in a herd. Simply walking behind them with a stick that you wave on the opposite side of where you want them to go guides them. They do, however, spook easily, so avoid sudden movements and loud noises around them.

In the wild, many geese mate for life, one of the few creatures (besides humans) that do. Domestic geese can be more like many of our favorite movie stars—serial monogamists, who mate with a single partner for a while and then move on.

## GETTING STARTED

Day-old ducklings and goslings rather than eggs you incubate are the best way to begin for novices. Get them in spring from a hatchery in your area, most of which are registered with the U.S. Department of Agriculture (your county extension office can also help you find them). If there are none near you, you can mail-order for them, too. Guinea fowl keets (as their hatchlings are known) are a little older when you get them, but they are very susceptible to cold and moisture. All of these little birds need extra protection and to be kept enclosed for a couple months until their reach mature size. Check the "Getting Started" section for chickens (page 158) for details on raising newborn domestic fowl.

# Rabbits

**You don't have to be like Farmer** McGregor battling Peter Rabbit to know that wild rabbits can be frustrating pests in your garden. They can mow down a row of lettuce overnight and take a nibble out of every strawberry. But domesticated bunnies are just the opposite. Keep them out of your garden and they can be a real asset to your diversified urban homestead. They're also lovable and easy to care for pets, perfect for small homes and where other kinds of livestock are not welcome. Just don't forget that rabbits earned their reputation for reproducing often and abundantly—be sure you have a plan for what to do when that happens.

## BENEFITS

Rabbits can't survive on leftover vegetable scraps (more on that in the feeding section below), but they do enjoy the parts of the food that you probably (hopefully) are tossing into the compost pile, such as carrot tops, potato peels, and apple cores. They turn that waste and all the other food you give them into potent pellets of fertilizer. Even better, rabbit manure is not as "hot" (or nitrogen-heavy) as poultry manure, so you can use it to feed plants in the ground or even in containers without composting it first.

Certain breeds of rabbit, such as the Angora types, grow fur that can be harvested without harm to the bunny and then spun into very soft yarn you can use to make hats, scarves, and other knitted items. Of course, if you are able to treat your rabbits more like livestock than pets, their pelts are highly prized, and their flesh is a healthy, low-fat meat.

## CHOOSING BREEDS

You have hundreds of choices that you can narrow down by considering your conditions and what you want the rabbits for. Netherland Dwarf and other miniature breeds grow only to about three and a half pounds, so you don't need a lot of room for them to live in and they eat considerably less than the larger breeds. Their litters are also smaller—usually only two to four kits at a time.

Slightly larger "small" breeds get to be about five pounds, still a manageable size for small properties. They come in a wide range of colors, from black to white to brown or gray. Many of them have floppy rather than upright ears. Dutch and Himalayan are two widely available breeds in this size range. The medium breeds, which get to be about seven pounds, include those with the Angora fur. Most of the popular breeds for showing, such as Mini Lop, American Sable, and Harlequin, come from this group. The larger giants can weigh as much as twenty-five pounds, so they're in demand by people who are raising them for fur or meat. Giant Chinchilla and Flemish Giant are two of the most commonly found.

## FEEDING

As you already know, rabbits love vegetables and fruits, but they need a more balanced selection of nutrients than they get from raw produce. Nearly everybody who raises rabbits successfully feeds them with packaged pellets based on alfalfa (for protein) blended with other ingredients chosen to give them the nourishment they need. Give them produce only as a treat, not a staple in their diet.

Each day a four-pound rabbit will eat about four ounces of pellets, or about one ounce per pound of their weight. Beware of overfeeding. Caged rabbits don't get the same amount of exercise as wild ones do, but they don't always regulate their food consumption accordingly. An overweight rabbit is not healthy or cute.

Your rabbits need roughage in their diet, and hay is the best way to give it to them. They can eat as much of it as they want, so provide them with a steady supply of timothy or other dried grass cut from fields you know were not treated with pesticides.

You can feed them from any dish with sides low enough for your bunnies to get their noses into it. Be sure the dish is stable, so they don't constantly turn it over and spill out all the food. Also, set up the feeding area so that the food stays dry. Soggy food can make them sick. Evening is the best time to feed rabbits, because they are more active at night than during the day. You can feed them in the morning, but whichever time you choose, be consistent. A routine helps rabbits stay happy and healthy.

Rabbits drink a lot of water because they cannot absorb it from the food they eat. Many people provide them with water bottles with spouts, like those designed for guinea pig cages. Most rabbits figure out how to use them, but because the bottles are relatively small, you may need to refill them more often than if you use a ceramic crock or just a dish designed for small dogs. Rabbits dehydrate quickly, so be sure they always have access to fresh, clean water.

## SHELTER

An attractive rabbit hutch is fairly easy to build, but whether you make or buy shelter for your rabbits, each bunny needs its own compartment—male rabbits (known as "bucks") and females ("does") fight each other, and two of the opposite sex will do what bunnies are known to do: reproduce. Give each rabbit at least three square feet of floor space and two feet of head space—more for larger breeds—so they have enough room to move around and stretch out.

If you build the cage from wire, don't use chicken mesh, which can hurt the rabbits' feet. Even better, provide a sitting board (about the size of their bodies) so they can rest in comfort. A wire floor is sensible, though, because it allows their waste to fall out, which makes cleaning easier. You can collect the bunny manure on a tarp beneath the hutch so you can use it in your garden or compost pile. Rabbits can chew through wood and plastic, so if you use those materials, be sure to reinforce them with wire to keep them from escaping. Many hutch designs feature a door that lets you get inside to clean, but those with a roof that opens instead are even easier to maintain.

Be sure to put the rabbit hutch where it will be shaded from the heat and shielded from cold winds. Get it up off the ground to keep their predators, most commonly dogs, from getting to them. If you want your rabbits to graze in your yard, you can set them up in a movable pen (like the chicken tractor I described on page 156). Early evening (around dusk) is a good time to let them graze each day.

## HABITS

People who keep rabbits as indoor pets have found that they can train them to use a litter box. If you do this and use standard kitty litter, don't put the used litter in your compost pile. The litter likely contains chemicals to fight odor and for other purposes that you don't want to put in your garden. Many bunnies that live in close quarters with people do become affectionate lap pets.

You might be surprised to know that rabbits do vocalize. Though we think of them as silent, they make low grunting noises when they are agitated, and they let out an unnervingly shrill scream when they are threatened and frightened or hurt. They grind their teeth softly when they are content, kind of like a kitten's purr.

## GETTING STARTED

The American Rabbit Breeders Association maintains a state-by-state listing of breeders, and that's the best place to start looking for a reputable source. I'm not saying you need a bunny with a pedigree, but an established breeder is the most reliable way to get what you pay for.

Whatever you do, don't try to catch wild rabbits and raise them in captivity. And if you decide to quit raising rabbits, find someone else to take them rather than releasing them into the wild. They retain their natural instincts, but without experience on their own, they won't last long.

# HASSENPFEFFER, ANYONE?

IN GERMANY, *HASSENPFEFFER*, OR RABBIT STEW, IS A POPULAR TRADITIONAL dish. Rabbit is enjoyed in other European countries and elsewhere where they are abundant. Rabbit as meat is no longer popular in North America, but as more people begin to question the sustainability of eating beef, pork, and chicken, it is gaining new enthusiasts. Here's why eco-conscious meat-eaters are considering rabbit.

- Rabbits eat food that people don't.

- They're easy to raise and to butcher (sorry, there's no better word) yourself.

- Since rabbits reproduce quickly, the supply can be constant.

- Rabbits are very efficient at converting calories into meat: rabbits can produce six pounds of edible meat from the same amount of food and water it takes a cow to produce one pound.

# Goats

**Grazing animals wouldn't seem** well suited to populated areas, but goats are highly adaptable and easy to manage in a limited space. If you have 3,000 square feet or more for a pen, you have enough room for a couple of goats. Though goats don't really eat tin cans (despite what you've seen in storybooks), they do feed eagerly on weeds and other undesirable plants, so they can graze in abandoned lots, along roadsides, and in just about any uncultivated space. Goats are generally docile, and some breeds are even friendly.

## BENEFITS

Did you know that outside North America, goat is the most commonly eaten red meat around the world? It is a staple of Caribbean cuisine, which you may have tried if you've ever been to the islands. But even if you don't want to raise goats to eat, dairy goats can supply you with highly nutritious milk that is easier to digest for those who are allergic to cow's milk. It's easy to turn goat's milk into chèvre and other fresh cheeses, or make it into yogurt and even ice cream. Angora and Cashmere goats grow the soft fur that is transformed into the highly valued fabric for which those names are famous. All breeds of goat are handy for mowing down grass and other vegetation, including thistle and other hard-to-eliminate weeds, without resorting to poisonous herbicides. In fact, goat owners in many places are renting out their herds for this very purpose. (See "Goats for Rent" on page 173.) As with other kinds of backyard livestock, goat manure is a nutrient-rich ingredient for your compost pile. Goat's milk soap is an expensive luxury that you could make yourself.

## CHOOSING BREEDS

Start by considering what you want goats for. Certain breeds are better suited to milk or meat production. La Mancha, Nubian, and French Alpine are the most common dairy goats, while Spanish and San Clemente are popular for meat. If you want goats for fiber, Angora and Cashmere are the best choices.

For a small backyard you can get miniature versions of many breeds, including the dairy types. They were created by cross-breeding Nigerian Dwarf goats with other breeds. They reach up to 100 pounds and still produce a substantial amount of milk. Mini La Manchas are widely recommended for urban goat herds because they are calm, quiet, productive, and (I'm not afraid to say it) kind of cute.

For your city or suburban backyard herd, stick with females (called "does" or "nannies") rather than males ("bucks" or "billys"). The boys can become aggressive and noisy when the girls are in heat, and they can have a very strong odor. Goats are social animals, so get at least two or more nannies.

## FEEDING

Goats want and need to graze, or rather to browse, meaning they prefer to munch on shrubs and the lower branches of trees rather than on grass and other ground covers, though they do eat grasses when they are available to them.

Along with the vegetation goats find on their own, give them roughage such as corn stalks or hay. Almost any kind of hay is fine, though hay from legumes like alfalfa, clover, and vetch is more nutritious than grass hay, like fescue or sudangrass. Alfalfa is especially desirable because it is rich in calcium, which helps with milk production. If you give your goats other types of hay, provide them with alfalfa pellets (simply ground up and dried alfalfa), which you can find at pet stores and feed mills. You can give your goats grain like corn or oats at times of the year when they don't have much to browse on, but don't rely on it because, like cows, they are ruminants evolved to turn green matter into milk. Experienced goat keepers also give them mineral supplements that contain copper, an essential nutrient for them. Be sure they have a steady supply of water to drink, too, especially during hot, dry spells.

## SHELTER

Cold is no problem for goats, but they are prone to catching pneumonia when they stay wet. A garage, a toolshed, or any structure you build that lets them go inside when it's raining or snowing works. Make sure the entrance is set up so they can come in and go out at will. If the structure is high enough for you to stand in, you will find it much easier to muck out the bedding.

Unless you live where there are long rainy periods, such as the Pacific Northwest, the ideal floor for your goat shelter is bare ground rather than wood or concrete, because soil absorbs much of the animals' waste, and the microbes living in the earth can decompose it. If the shelter does have a solid floor, cover it with wood shavings or straw to absorb the waste. And remember to clean out the floor covering and replace it with fresh material once a month or so. Add the dirty old material to your compost pile.

Goats find surprisingly ingenious ways to escape from a fence. Chain-link is the most secure, but if that costs more than you can spend to enclose their pen, you can use wire or stock fencing that's at least four feet high. The gate must be sturdy and secure, and try to set it up so

that the latch is on the outside—goats have been known to figure those out, too.

My neighbor has always kept a wooden picnic table or low flatbed wagon in his goats' pen. I frequently see the goats chasing each other on and off these platforms in what looks a lot like the game of "King of the Mountain" we used to play on dirt piles around the house where I grew up. I'm not sure exactly what they're doing, and neither is my neighbor, but it does seem like they get a lot of exercise out of it.

## HABITS

The best way to ensure that dairy goats continuously produce milk is to breed them each year. Rather than keep your own billy goat, take your nannies to a farm that can provide a billy for this purpose. Most experts say you must stop milking while they're pregnant, but you can start again shortly after the kids are born.

You don't need special machinery to milk goats—you can do it by hand—but a milking platform they stand on while you sit and aim the stream into a container makes the job much easier. You can milk your goats daily for the ten months or so that they are lactating between pregnancies. Depending on the breed, they produce an average of about three quarts of milk a day.

Goats are subject to occasional infestations by intestinal worms. You can find organic (herbal) deworming formulas online and nowadays at many feed stores or from farm animal veterinarians.

## GETTING STARTED

If you know of a county or local 4-H club fair, that is the best place to look for goats to buy. You might also ask at a nearby feed store about people who come in to buy supplies for goats. Wherever you find the goats, be sure they have clear eyes, a straight back, and a wide, deep chest.

## GOATS FOR RENT

IN A TWENTY-FIRST CENTURY MASH-UP of high-tech and good old-fashioned, two of the best-known brands on the Internet have hired goats to help manage the landscape outside their offices. Google and Yahoo are just two of the many businesses and individuals who lease a herd of goats to clear brush from their properties. Goats are an increasingly popular and eco-friendly solution for cleaning up land overgrown with weeds, brambles, and other unwanted vegetation. They're especially valuable on steep slopes and other places where people and machines don't work so well.

How much can a small a herd of goats earn? From $200 to $1,000 or more per day, depending on the scope of the job and the number of goats needed to do it. If you want to put your goats to work, you'll also need a portable electric fence or a couple of well-trained herding dogs to ensure that your workers don't wander off the job.

# KNOW THE CODE

THE FIRST AND MOST IMPORTANT QUESTION YOU NEED TO ANSWER BEFORE YOU start raising any livestock is: what are the local regulations about keeping animals where you live? Just fifty or sixty years ago, few municipalities restricted homeowners' rights to keep bees, chickens, or ducks. But as the power of neighborhood associations grew and people became more removed from the source of their food, laws were passed to prohibit raising even these pet-size animals in many cities and the suburbs. Today, the tide is reversing and these laws are being revoked.

Still, you need to check first. Start with your local zoning board, where these laws typically originate. Your county extension office is a reliable source of information, too.

Even if you are permitted to raise any of these animals where you live, take the time to inform your neighbors about what you are doing and explain all the measures you will take to keep the animals from becoming a nuisance. Pay particular attention to making sure the animals are out of their sight and won't produce unwelcome odors. Oh, and bring along a jar of honey or a carton of eggs to help convey the tangible benefits of their tolerance.

# BUY A SHARE

DO YOU LIVE IN A PLACE WHERE KEEPING ANY LIVESTOCK IS NOT FEASIBLE? That does not mean you have to settle for eggs and meat from factory-scale operations (I can't even call these places "farms"). You can buy locally produced, pasture-raised animal products at many farmers' markets and even in some of the progressive-minded grocers like Whole Foods Market.

Another way to get more safely and humanely produced eggs and meat is to join a CSA (a community-supported agriculture farm) that specializes in these items. You buy a "subscription" at the start of the season and get a share of the harvest each week. You also share with the farmers in the risks of agriculture.

In an even simpler arrangement, some small farmers offer shares of their livestock to a few people, who make a down payment on the meat when the season starts and collect after the butchering. One year our family purchased a quarter of a steer—from a small herd of about a dozen raised on pasture not far from our house in the suburbs—which was delivered to us in the form of the best-tasting steaks, roasts, and ground beef we've ever had at home. We needed a large freezer to keep it all, but at $2.25 per pound for all cuts, we easily justified the cost of the freezer. This year we've invested in a half share of a hog and are already looking forward to the best chops, ribs, and tenderloin imaginable.

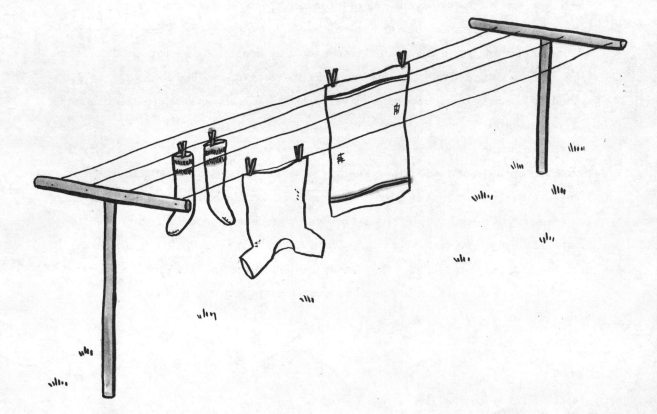

# CHAPTER FIVE

# CARING FOR THE HOME

**Y**ou're not planning to move out of your house or apartment and into a log cabin or yurt, but you would like to be more self-sufficient and use our precious resources wisely. You can become less dependent on products and services and enjoy the money savings and satisfaction that come with providing for at least some of your own needs. Whether you need to get rid of refuse, wash your clothes, water your plants, or deal with a pest problem, the solution may be right in your backyard.

# Waste Management

**Grass, leaves, and other yard waste,** along with discarded food scraps, constitute a quarter of the stuff that gets hauled off to landfills in the United States. That's just wasteful and unnecessary when all of us can be managing that refuse ourselves. Whether you live in a single-family home or an apartment, you can turn almost any kind of garbage that was once a plant into compost. Don't worry about what you'll do with the compost—it just continues to break down and eventually is absorbed into the soil. If you have a garden or houseplants, you'll be glad to have the compost, the most effective fertilizer and soil conditioner known to man.

Growing and cooking your own food is work, but it can also be fun and very satisfying. Dealing with the garbage that's left over, not so much. Cleaning up after dinner may be a chore, but when you take kitchen scraps and other waste from around your home and yard and turn them into compost, you close the loop on the production-consumption cycle, reduce your contribution to overflowing landfills, and make fertilizer for the food plants you are growing. Most exciting—and I really mean most exciting—you get to participate in the nearly magical process that regenerates what's thrown away into a treasure gardeners call "black gold": rich, crumbly, sweet-smelling compost. You watch decomposition happen, and you will be fascinated.

You don't need special ingredients, a lot of space, or unique knowledge or skills to do this. You have the basic ingredients of compost around your home, regardless of where you live. You can set up a compost pile in a space as small as 3 feet by 3 feet. But even if you don't have enough space for a compost pile, you can make it on a patio or balcony in a container that's the size of a standard trash can, or even in a box you keep underneath your kitchen sink. Just about all that is required of you is patience.

## WHY COMPOST (*Wherever You Live*)

1. Composting is like alchemy, transforming banana peels, apple cores, and coffee grounds into black gold—aka the best plant fertilizer imaginable.

2. Landfills are a dirty, stinking mess—no place for innocent kitchen scraps.

3. Your corner of the world stays a little bit cleaner.

4. You need no special skills or knowledge—just toss garbage into a heap and let it rot.

5. It keeps earthworms fat and happy, and don't they deserve that?

## WHAT IS COMPOST?

Let's start with a little science. Everything that was once alive eventually decomposes. Billions of microbes, such as bacteria and fungi, feed on decaying tissue, breaking it down into smaller pieces as they digest it. Those microbes show up and get to work almost the moment the living thing dies. When the decomposing matter was once a plant, the stuff the microbes leave behind when they are done digesting is compost. This process occurs continuously in nature, in every meadow, forest, and vacant lot, without people getting involved at all. That's what the slogan "Compost Happens" means.

*Humus*, a word commonly used as a synonym for compost, is more accurately applied to organic (that is, once living) matter in the process of decay. So, for instance, a pile of leaves that are starting to break down, but are still recognizable as leaves, is humus. Helpful stuff for building healthy soil, but not as valuable as compost.

When compost is finished breaking down, it looks like the crumbs left behind after you cut a slice of chocolate cake—dark brown bits with a lightly sweet, earthy smell. If you squeeze those bits in the palm of your hand, they clump together, but if you crumble them with your fingers, they fall apart. At its finished state, the original ingredients are no longer discernible, and the compost is teeming with microbes.

## MAKING COMPOST

As I said, nature makes compost without any effort by people. If your only goal is to dispose of your own waste, you don't need to do much other than to pile it up. Later on in this chapter, I'll tell you about what should and should not go into your compost pile.

You can take an active role in the process to speed it up, keep it functioning efficiently, and produce a richer, more balanced fertilizer to use in growing your food. You do this by choosing and mixing the ingredients thoughtfully and ensuring that the microbes have the air and moisture they need to keep working steadily.

The basic formula is very simple. Fresh ingredients like banana peels, carrot tops, and other kitchen scraps are high in nitrogen and are referred to as "greens." Older, drier stuff, such as fallen leaves or straw,

are carbon-rich "brown" ingredients. The ideal blend for compost is three parts brown to one part green, but don't worry about making that too exact—just remember that you need some of each type, with generally more brown than green—to get your pile to decompose evenly.

- *To build a compost pile,* **find a level spot that's nine square feet. The closer it is to your kitchen or garden, the more use it will get. The spot does not need to get direct, full sun, but some sun each day can help keep it warm and active on cold days.**
- *Cover the ground* **on the spot with a couple-inch-thick layer of straw. If you don't have access to straw, you can use six to eight sheets of black-and-white newspaper (no glossy color pages) instead.**
- *Cover that with* **a layer of green material.**
- *Continue to add* **greens and browns as you have them.**
- *Moisten the ingredients* **if they are very dry.**

## MANAGING A COMPOST PILE

You gradually build your compost pile, adding ingredients as you get them. When the pile reaches three feet high, it will have enough volume to begin "cooking." That is, it will heat up (from the microbes' activity) on the inside and get warm enough that you can actually see steam coming from it on cool mornings. When the stuff on the inside of the pile has finished cooking and looks decomposed—two to three weeks after you built the pile—you want to move the inside of the pile to the outside and move the stuff on the outside to the center. You do this by digging out the center with a shovel or a garden fork and then pushing the outside material into the center. This process is known as "turning" the compost pile.

You can, and want to, keep adding fresh material to your compost pile. When the air is very dry—especially in winter and during a spell of windy days—moisten but do not soak the pile. The microbes need air (which you give them when you turn the pile) and moisture to function efficiently.

Sometimes you will find yourself with a lot of one type of ingredient, such as fallen leaves or grass clippings. Instead of dumping it all into your compost pile at once, bag or stockpile them near your pile (if possible) and add them gradually as you accumulate other mix-ins. A diverse mix of materials makes the best compost and the easiest-to-manage pile.

## RAW MATERIALS

Almost anything that comes from a plant can go into the compost pile. With just a couple exceptions I'll tell you about in this section, no animal products belong in your compost pile. We'll look at the greens (high nitrogen) and browns (high carbon), which doesn't refer to their color but rather to their state of freshness.

### GREEN INGREDIENTS

*Kitchen scraps.* Only from fruits and vegetables, such as apple cores and onion skins.

*Grass clippings.* From lawns that have not been treated with synthetic fertilizers, herbicides, or other chemicals.

*Garden waste.* Everything from tomato vines that you have finished harvesting to pulled weeds that have not gone to seed

*Herbivore manure.* The waste from chickens, cows, horses, rabbits, guinea pigs, and other herbivores are one of the most nutrient-rich ingredients you can add to your compost. (Yes, manure is brown, but it's so nitrogen-rich that it falls in the "green" column.) The bedding from stables—the mixture of straw and dung—is an almost perfect addition to the pile.

*Coffee grounds.* (Brown again, but they belong here for the same reason.)

*Human and pet hair (any color).* They're rich in nitrogen and are easy to get from barbers and groomers. Add them in small amounts because they break down slowly.

## BROWN INGREDIENTS

*Fallen leaves.* The more you shred them (with a lawn mower, for instance), the faster they will decompose.

*Straw.* Be sure you don't get hay instead. Straw is the hollow stems left behind after corn or other grain crops are harvested. Hay is simply cut dry grasses, and it can include the seedheads. You don't want those seeds in your pile because they will sprout up as weeds wherever you use the compost.

*Shredded paper.* Black-and-white newsprint and office paper can be used as carbon-rich brown materials, but shred them up first so they don't clump up in your compost pile. Cardboard is better as a weed-block in a new garden or pathway.

*Sawdust.* It is so carbon-dense that it breaks down very slowly, so use it in moderation. Never use sawdust from treated or painted wood.

*Woodstove or fireplace ash.* A rich source of the important plant nutrient potassium, ashes are highly alkaline. Add only small amounts—a bucketful or so—at a time.

*Eggshells.* One key exception to the "no animal products" rule of thumb. Eggshells add calcium to your compost, and while they decompose slowly, you can almost watch the fragile shells breaking into ever smaller pieces.

## THE "NEVER EVER" LIST

These items do not belong in your compost pile, because they could introduce harmful diseases or toxins, or because they won't degrade fully.

*Meats, dairy products, bones, and fish.* They decompose slowly, make your compost smell bad, and attract animals.

*Dog, cat, pig, and reptile manures (and bedding from their living quarters).* They often contain parasites or dangerous pathogens that are harmful to humans, particularly pregnant women, children, and people with compromised immune systems. Never put them in your compost pile.

*Human manure.* Bad idea, in case you are wondering. Do you know what's in that $#!+?

*Glossy paper.* High-quality colored paper is printed with colored ink that contains heavy metals. Black-and-white newspaper is safe.

*Diseased plants.* Toss them as far as possible from your garden, put them in the garbage, or burn them. If they get into your compost, they could spread the disease when you use it in your garden.

*Gypsum board scraps.* Gypsum is a natural mineral, but the building material may contain paint and other undesirable toxins.

## LOCAL RESOURCES

You probably have many of these ingredients around the house, and they're the efficient way to start your compost pile. But you don't have to stop there. No matter where you live, you can scavenge for many more valuable ingredients that will make your compost pile work better and the results be more nutritious for your garden plants.

*Zoos, animal parks, and pet stores.* Don't live near a farm or stable? Bring a container with a tight-fighting lid to other places where plant-eating animals are kept. Almost any of them will gladly share a load or two with you, especially if you offer to shovel it yourself.

*Restaurants and cafeterias.* Every day they're generating pounds and pounds of fruit and vegetable scraps. If you know someone in the trade or just have no inhibition about asking for the waste, provide a lidded container and pick it up often.

*Food processors.* Manufacturing plants that turn freshly harvested produce into food products throw away tons of useful ingredients.

*Landscapers.* Lawn-care services and other landscaping pros collect and must dispose of grass clippings, tree prunings, and the like almost every day. Many of them will deliver the stuff to your home if you take it off their hands.

*Parks department.* Another source for grass clippings and leaves for your compost pile. Whenever you get grass clippings from an outside source, try to stay away from any that have been treated with herbicides, which may kill friendly microbes in your compost pile.

*Neighborhood watch.* Believe it or not, people throw away valuable compost ingredients. Go down a street in an older neighborhood—where the trees are tall—on trash night, and you will see bags and bags of leaves by the curb. Would anyone miss them if you helped yourself to a few of them for your compost pile? Talk about an embarrassment of riches.

## CONTAINING COMPOST

You don't need a dedicated composter. You can just pile up the ingredients and let them decompose. But if you live close to your neighbors or just like neatness and order (you know who you are), then you'll want a compost bin that keeps the ingredients discreetly inside and scavenging animals outside. If you want to buy one, there are lots of different designs you can choose from, online (try Composters.com) and at most home and garden centers. Most fall into one of two categories:

## BOX DESIGN

Four sides and a lid, but no bottom, these bins are generally made from wood or plastic (often recycled). Be sure to choose one that has ventilation openings on the sides to allow air and moisture to move through the pile. Many have a little door in the front to allow you easier access to the finished compost.

*Benefits:* Worms and other soil-dwellers can easily get into the pile from below and begin helping with the decomposition.

*Considerations:* You need nine square feet of ground space to site it. You must turn the pile with a shovel or fork.

## SPIN DESIGN

Sometimes called the "Tumbler" type of compost bin, this design has a large container, like a barrel, mounted on a rack. You put the ingredients inside the barrel and then spin it to mix and aerate them. These can range from the size of a small trashcan to as big as an oil drum. Because your ingredients have no access to the ground, you need to add a little soil to the bin to introduce the right microbes for healthy decomposition.

*Benefits:* Ideal for patios, balconies, and other places where there is no bare ground. Very easy—fun even—to turn.

*Considerations:* Makes compost slowly unless you fill it up all at once, turn it regularly, and add nothing more. No contact with the soil—you need to add finished compost or garden soil to spur decomposition. Dries out quickly.

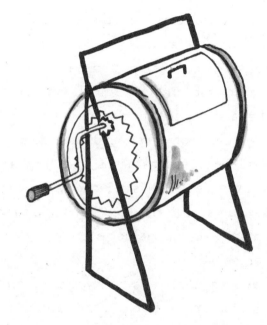

## COMPOST FOR SALE

Many municipalities give away compost to residents. But if yours doesn't or you need a small amount for a container garden, you can buy bags of it at nurseries and home centers.

Before you buy, check the bag. Though manure is often in well-made compost, you don't want composted manure. It is too rich for containers and doesn't have the balance of nutrients as you get in compost made with a variety of ingredients. Also beware of bags that list "biosolids" as an ingredient. That is an industry term for sewage sludge, and you don't want to spread it on your garden or put it in your containers.

Ask an employee where you are shopping for compost if you can see a sample. It should smell sweet and earthy, not sour or moldy. Squeeze it in your fist. If it clumps into a hard ball, it's too soggy. If it doesn't form a ball, it's too old, dry, and dusty. You want compost that sticks together from a gentle squeeze and falls apart when you rub it between your fingers. Be sure there are no discernible big chunks of ingredi-ents that haven't decomposed in the bag.

## USING COMPOST

Although you continually add fresh ingredients to your compost pile, it stays the same size because it's always breaking them down. So you don't have to do anything with your compost—you can just use it as a way to dispose of your own waste (and feel good about that). But it is the best fertilizer you can use in your garden, and it improves many of your soil's qualities in the process. These ideas will help you get started.

*Seed-starting mix.* When planting seeds in pots indoors before moving them outside, blend three parts peat moss or coir with one part compost. Use your most finished compost for this.

*Container mix.* Instead of potting soil, make the mix half peat or coir and half compost. The finer the particles in the compost, the better.

*In the garden.* Spread a half-inch layer of compost on top of the soil before planting and once or twice during the growing season. Scratch it in lightly to the top few inches. Or add a handful or two to each hole when you're transplanting seedlings.

*Compost tea.* Brew up a batch of this nutrient-rich liquid fertilizer for feeding potted plants. To make it, put a shovelful or two in a burlap bag or old pillowcase. Tie the bag shut and steep it in a bucket of water for two to three days. Dilute the "tea" with an equal amount of water, and sprinkle on your plants. Spread the compost that's left in the bag in your garden, or toss it back into the compost pile.

## THREE BASIC BINS

You can make your own compost bin with materials that are easy to salvage.

*Wire ring:* To make a three-foot diameter compost bin, get ten feet of chicken wire or other light metal fencing. Form the wire into a circle. Fasten the ends together with zip ties or twine. Be careful with wire ends—they are very sharp and prone to poking you when you're not paying attention. Set up on the ground and fill, starting with a layer of straw.

*Pallet box:* Many businesses that receive large shipments give wooden pallets to anybody who will haul them away. Set three of them on their ends and form them into three sides of a cube. Cinch them together—at the top, middle, and bottom—with zip ties. With the fourth side, secure only one side so that it can still open like a gate to make it easy for you to shovel out the finished compost. You can also use snow fencing or plastic mesh and metal posts for the sides of compost bin.

*Trash Can Tumbler:* If you have enough space for a garbage can, you have room for this composter. Find or buy a 32 gallon or larger plastic garbage can with a tight-fighting lid. Drill two- to three-inch holes about six to twelve inches apart all the way around the sides of the trash can. Cover the holes with hardware cloth or window screening, and secure with duct tape. Fill the can with your raw ingredients. Once a week or so, lay the can on its side and roll it back and forth a few times, holding your hand on the lid to be sure it doesn't pop open, to "turn" your compost.

## KITCHEN COMPOST

If you have no room for even a trash can, you can still make compost. All you need is a cool, dark spot where you can keep a plastic storage container—like under your kitchen sink or in a closet. That's where the worms will live as they dispose of your fruit and vegetable scraps, along with newspaper and small amounts of yard waste.

Vermicomposting, or composting with worms, doesn't produce a lot of compost to use in your garden, though the black liquid you get is super-rich in nutrients and an ideal fertilizer for container plants.

To make your own worm bin, get an eight- to ten-gallon plastic storage box with a lid and drill twenty quarter-inch holes in the bottom. These let condensation drain out—you can use a second lid as a tray to catch the small amount of moisture that comes out. Around the top edge of the box, drill ventilation holes about an inch apart. Drill twenty-five to thirty holes in the lid, too.

The worms need bedding. Make that by cutting newspaper into inch-wide strips and moistening (not soaking) it. Cover the bottom of the bin with a three- to four-inch thick layer. Add brown leaves or a scoop of soil, if you can get some.

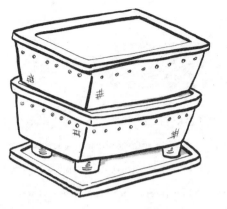

You can buy worms online or through bait shops, or you can capture them in the wild. Look under leaf piles or lure them in by setting a piece of wet cardboard on your lawn overnight—the worms will be underneath in the morning.

You can feed your worms any fruit and vegetable kitchen scraps, like apple cores and broccoli stalks. And add them gradually to prevent the food from rotting before the worms have a chance to digest it. Just like with any composting, don't put meat, fish, or dairy products in your worm bin. Give the worms fresh, damp newspaper once a week or so.

Store the bin in a well-ventilated area away from direct sunlight, high heat, or frigid cold.

After a few months, the bedding will have broken down into rough compost—brown and chunky. Time to add new bedding. Move the old pile to one side of the bin and make a pile of new bedding and garbage on the other. In a week or two the worms will have moved to the new pile and you can remove the old compost. It's ready to use in your garden.

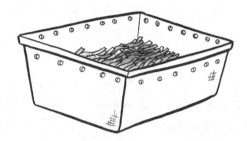

Black liquid, or "worm tea," collects in the bottom tray and inside the container. It is a pure liquid fertilizer. You can collect it with a baster or just pour it into a cup. Add a couple tablespoons to your watering can when you water your container plants.

If your bin smells like rotting garbage, you're adding food too fast for the worms to consume it. Hold off on giving them more. If your bin smells like mold, you've made the newspaper too soggy—add some that's dry.

Fruit flies are a problem when you don't bury the food waste in the newspaper or you have too much food for the worms to handle.

# PET POO COMPOSTER

WASTE FROM YOUR DOG OR CAT (OR YOURSELF, FOR THAT MATTER) IS BIO-DEG-radable, but it is not safe to put in your compost pile. Manure (that's a nice technical word for it, isn't it?) from carnivores may contain parasites and disease-carrying microbes that can survive the decomposition process and infest your garden vegetables and fruit when you use the compost. You can and should put waste from plant-eating pets, such as guinea pigs, gerbils, and parakeets, in your compost pile.

Throwing dog and cat waste into the trash where it will be carried off to a landfill isn't ideal either. Pet poop wrapped up in plastic is held in a kind of suspended animation and clogs up already over-flowing landfills. Left to decompose wherever it falls, dog doo is not only a stinking mess, it also may wash into streams and reservoirs, depositing its load of disease vectors into the water supply. You can flush dog and cat waste (though not plastic bags or kitty litter) down the toilet and send it off to your septic tank or a municipal water treatment plant. Another, more resourceful solution that will appeal to many homesteaders is a "dog doo digester." You can buy one, but it's so easy to make that you ought to at least consider trying to set up your own first.

1. Start by looking for a location where you can dig that's far from your food garden and any aboveground water supply. An out-of-the-way place is best, so no neighbors see what you're doing, even if it is completely safe and will be odor-free.

2. Get a small plastic trash can or a large plastic bin with a lid. Drill or poke eight to ten small holes in the sides, near the bottom. Cut a wide opening at the bottom—a keyhole saw makes this quick and easy.

3. Dig a hole that the container fits in completely.

4. Make a base layer of small rocks or gravel at the bottom of the hole. The container

should rest on the base so that it sits a couple inches above ground level and allows the lid to be put on snugly.

5. Backfill dirt around the outside of the container to hold the container firmly in the hole.

That's all there is to it. To use it, lift the lid and drop the poop into the bin. Add carbon-rich materials such as sawdust, fallen leaves, dried grass clippings, or shredded paper. If you prefer, you can also add a natural septic starter (found in hardware stores and home centers). Replace the lid. The waste slowly degrades, liquefies, and drains away. You don't need to empty the container ever.

This system works best if you are scooping up the waste and adding it to the bin directly. If you pick up your pet's poop with a bag, look for cornstarch-based bags, which are now widely available at pet stores and online. Standard bags won't degrade in the digester, so if you use those, you need to empty their contents into the container and then toss the bag in the trash.

# Water

**The earth's surface is three-quar-**ters water, as you probably remember from science class, but did you know that less than 3% of that is fresh water? To put it another way, if all the world's water were fit into a gallon jug, the fresh water available for us to use would equal only about one tablespoon. It is a most precious resource—after just three days without it, you die. For most of us, water streams out of a tap when we need it, and we give it no more thought than whether it is cold or hot. We rely on it not only to hydrate ourselves, but for so many other things from cleaning our bodies, our clothes, and our homes to irrigating our gardens and orchards.

As a resourceful homesteader, you want to use water as efficiently as possible, whether it comes from your own well or a municipal reservoir. If you think about it, you can probably come up with lots of ways to save water in your home, but I want to share a few ideas and reminders that I think are especially relevant for homesteaders.

## INSIDE

You can save a lot of water just by paying attention to when the spigot is on. Do all you can to keep water from simply running straight down the drain and always think efficiency. Here are a few places to start.

- Put a bucket in the tub to collect the water that comes out of the spigot while you're waiting for it to warm up enough for you to shower or bathe. Use that water on your garden or houseplants.
- Take the same approach with water you use for rinsing fruits and vegetables.
- Keep a pitcher of water in your refrigerator rather than letting it run from the tap until it's cool enough to be refreshing.
- Soak used pots and pans instead of trying to scrape them clean while the water runs.
- A fully loaded dishwasher uses water more efficiently than washing by hand while the water runs. If you have two sinks in your kitchen, you can wash by hand efficiently if you use one side for soaking and one for rinsing.
- Consider replacing older shower heads

with newer, low-flow models. If you have an older toilet, replace it with a newer, high-efficiency type. Or retrofit it with a low-cost dual flush kit that lets you choose between a simple rinse for liquids or a full flush for solids.

• Showering with a partner can be not only water wise but also fun—as long as you don't get too distracted in the process and end up staying in the shower longer.

Gray water is water that's been used in your house to wash you, dishes, or clothes (as opposed to blackwater, which comes from the toilet or garbage disposal). Gray water typically constitutes 50% or more of the water that goes down the drain in your home. In many areas you are permitted to set up a system to reuse gray water for irrigating your garden, washing your car, and otherwise using outdoors. In some places you can even use gray water for toilet flushing.

Recycling gray water can dramatically reduce your demand for fresh water and help you to be more self-sufficient. Gray water does, however, contain bacteria and other microbes that pose some risks to your health. It needs to be filtered through a system that's designed to clean it sufficiently for reuse. You can find kits and plans online, but if you are not adept and experienced at basic plumbing, bring in an expert to help you get your system set up properly. Check out the resources section of this book for leads on how to get started.

## OUTSIDE

I know you remember some of these recommendations from the gardening chapter, but I have to reiterate them here because they're so important to water conservation.

• Keep a layer of natural mulch on your garden and around your landscaping plants at all times, but especially in summer. Mulch keeps the bright sun from evaporating all the moisture from the soil and prevents water-sucking weeds from putting down roots. Grass clippings, shredded leaves, and straw are free (or low-cost), effective mulches for your vegetable garden. If you need a more attractive mulch for flower beds, trees, and shrubs, bark chips look nice and work well.

- Before you water your garden or flower beds, do the test on page 29. Once established, trees and shrubs do not need to be watered. If you find that those landscape plants are persistently dehydrated, they are not right for your conditions and you should move them to a spot that is better suited to them or replace them with varieties that are well-adapted to where you live.

- If you need to water your garden, do it in the morning (best time) or about an hour before sunset (next best time). If you water in the middle of the day, it will evaporate before the plants have a chance to take it up. Water directly to the roots—leaves do not absorb much moisture. Once the plants are established, soak the soil deeply once a week rather than sprinkling it daily. This encourages plants to grow deep roots, which can find moisture underground rather than in quicker-to-dry-out surface areas.

- A drip irrigation system is the most efficient way to water your garden. If you can't buy one, a soaker hose which "weeps" water along its length is the next best choice.

## RAIN BARREL

The best water for irrigating your garden falls from the sky. A rain barrel captures precipitation from a downspout and stores it until you need it. You can buy one or make your own with these basic instructions.

**1.** At a local restaurant, cafeteria, or supermarket ask for a food-grade plastic barrel—55 gallons is a common size, though a bigger one works fine if you get one. Be sure it has not been used to store chemicals or petroleum products. It should have a lid that opens readily and closes tightly.

**2.** Thoroughly clean the interior of the barrel. A simple solution of water, dish soap, and vinegar is very effective at killing unwelcome bacteria left in the barrel.

**3.** With a one-inch spade bit, hand drill a hole about eight inches from the bottom of the barrel.

**4.** Install a garden hose valve in the hole by placing the adapter and washer inside the barrel and the spigot on the outside (it helps

to have two people working together on this). Wrap the valve threads with Teflon plumbing tape to ensure a watertight fit. Tighten it slowly and gently to avoid cracking the barrel.

**5.** Drill another hole, the same size, near the top of the barrel. Install another hose valve or simple hose bib. With a hose attached, this will manage any overflow.

**6.** Get a skimmer basket like those used in garden ponds and swimming pools to filter out leaves and other debris. Trace the outline of the basket's bottom on the barrel's lid. With a keyhole saw or jigsaw, cut out the traced area. Cover the basket with window screen or hardware cloth to prevent mosquitoes and other disease-carrying insects from getting into the barrel. Set the basket into the hole.

**7.** Use sheet-metal snips or a hacksaw to cut off your downspout about three and half feet above the top of the barrel. Get an off-set diverter—available at home centers and building supply stores—and install it in the downspout. It functions as a splitter, allowing you to direct water into your rain barrel or out the bottom of the downspout.

**8.** Attach a flexible downspout extender into one side of the diverter and the cut-off piece of downspout into the other side.

**9.** Set the barrel on cinder blocks or bricks. Make it high enough for you to get a watering can easily underneath the hose valve.

**10.** Direct the flexible downspout extender into the skimmer basket. Check the forecast for rain.

# Housekeeping

**Television commercials would have** you believe that you need a specially formulated product to keep each surface in your home free of deadly germs and the dirt and grime that cause nearly fatal embarrassment. No one believes advertising tells the truth, but chances are you have a lot of these products around your house. Unfortunately, those products almost always are made with powerful chemicals that are poisonous to people and (in their manufacturing) toxic to the environment.

Do you have to choose between keeping your home sanitary and polluting the planet? Definitely not. A resourceful homesteader can use a few safe, ordinary household items to thoroughly clean just about every corner of the house, saving money and ensuring that kids and pets are not exposed to poisons in the process.

**White vinegar** (distilled) is a mild acid that breaks down dried-on dirt, mold and mildew, soap scum, and hard water deposits. Yes, the smell may remind you of salad dressing, but to me that's more tolerable than the fake floral scents used to cover up the noxious odor of chemicals in so many cleaning products. The aroma of vinegar is gone when you rinse with water after cleaning. For most uses, dilute vinegar about two to one with water. You can use more potent solutions, even straight vinegar, for really resistant dirt on durable surfaces like sinks and toilets, countertops and tile. Straight vinegar and hot water unclog bathtub drains without damaging pipes.

**Rubbing (isopropyl) alcohol** is a solvent that loosens grease and sticky stuff like hairspray and hardened toothpaste. Alcohol evaporates quickly without streaking, so it leaves glass and chrome shiny and smudge-free. Mix it with equal parts water and white vinegar, put the solution in a spray bottle, and forget about buying the blue window cleaner ever again.

**Baking soda** not only keeps your refrigerator smelling fresh, it is an abrasive, so you can use it to scrub stovetops, tubs and toilets, pots and pans, or almost any surface that needs a bit of elbow grease. Sprinkle baking soda on a damp sponge and then scrub away. For extra-resistant grime, make a thick paste with baking soda and a little water, and apply it to the dirty spot. Let it sit for about fifteen to twenty minutes—baking soda is an alkali that softens the stuck-on dirt—and then wipe clean. If your carpets and rugs smell musty, sprinkle baking soda on them, let sit for about three hours, then vacuum well.

**Hydrogen peroxide**, known as $H_2O_2$ to your chemistry teacher, is a very safe disinfectant. How safe? You can mix it half and half with water and gargle with it to kill germs in your mouth. (Just be sure you're using 3% hydrogen peroxide, which is the most commonly sold concentration. Also, spit it out—don't swallow it.) In your bathroom wipe mildew-stained tile grout with hydrogen peroxide, let sit for ten minutes, and come back to rinse it clean. Use hydrogen peroxide to clean cutting boards and countertops and protect them from salmonella and other bacteria.

**Liquid dish soap** is a mild detergent that is strong enough to clean hardwood and linoleum floors, walls, and other surfaces where you don't want to harm the paint or finish. Mix a tablespoon into a half-gallon of warm water until it dissolves thoroughly. Soak a soft rag (old T-shirts and underwear serve the purpose) in the solution, wring out the liquid until the rag is damp not dripping, and wipe the surfaces.

**Vegetable oil**, such as olive or canola, shines up furniture and other wood surfaces without leaving behind the waxy residue that commercial sprays do. Mix a cup of the oil with a half-cup of lemon juice, a mild acid that breaks down glass rings and smudges. Dab a little at a time on your cleaning rag, then rub it into the wood. Wait about five minutes, then wipe with a fresh rag to soak up any oil that doesn't soak into the wood. Polish wood like this every three to four months or so. For weekly dusting, use a cloth diaper, an old sock, or a piece of another fabric with static for the dust to cling to.

**Essential oils** are very potent and fragrant liquids made by distilling the leaves, stems, and roots of plants. Oils from eucalyptus, peppermint, or lavender give your homemade cleaners an authentic fresh scent and they're natural disinfectants. You can find essential oils in natural foods stores. They can be pricey, but you use only a few drops at a time.

Word of caution: My wife and I use the homemade cleaners I've shared with you here in our house, and they are gentle and effective. But I always suggest that you test them in your home first by using them in a small, discreet way so that if they are going to cause any damage to a surface, you discover that before you've used them everywhere.

If you decide to do away with toxic commercial cleaners, don't just simply toss them in the trash. Take them to a hazardous waste collection site in your area where they can be disposed of without harming the environment.

## LAUNDRY

The homesteaders of yesteryear had to heat water over a fire, soak their clothes in a tub, scrub them with bars of soap on a washboard, and hang them to dry outside or in front of the fire. Today, we have washing machines that heat their own water and agitate to remove dirt, fossil fuel (gas or electric) powered dryers, and an aisle full of different products to choose from to ensure the clothes are clean, smell fresh, and are free of the scourge of static. And if we are not fortunate enough to have these appliances in our homes, we can take our clothes to coin-operated laundries (or washaterias) that now have TVs, Wi-Fi access to the Internet, and in some cases, even bars serving cocktails.

Now, before you turn the page, let me assure you that I'm not about to suggest that you dump the appliances and pick up a washboard. But since the washer and dryer consume a lot of energy and the average household cleans 400 loads of laundry a year, I want to offer you ideas for reducing the costs to you and the environment.

## SIMPLE DETERGENT

The laundry detergent aisle in supermarkets and megacenters are lined with dozens of products sporting brilliant labels that suggest mountain streams and fresh breezes. Most of them, though, are brews of harsh chemicals and laboratory-formulated fragrances. Those that contain phosphates are especially damaging to our freshwater supplies and aquatic life. They are all toxic to people and pets, and are not essential. You can make your own safe and effective laundry detergent with water and three simple ingredients you can find tucked away in the corner of those cleaning-product aisles.

Start by picking up a bar of plain, unscented soap (such as Ivory or Fels Naptha), a box of washing soda (similar to baking soda, but it is sodium carbonate rather than sodium bicarbonate), and borax.

1. Grate a third to a half bar of the soap into a saucepan on your stove.

2. Add six cups of water and heat it until the soap melts.

3. Mix in a half-cup each of the washing soda and borax, and stir until it is all dissolved. Turn off the heat.

4. Pour four cups of hot water (from the tap—no need to heat it) into a bucket with a lid that holds at least two gallons. If you don't have one, you can get one from a restaurant or other food-service operation.

5. Add the soap mixture to the water and stir well. Add an additional gallon of hot water and stir again. If you want the detergent to have a pleasant scent, mix in a teaspoon or two of essential oil like lemon or lavender.

6. Let the soap sit for about twenty-four hours, and it will become the consistency of thick soup.

7. You can pour it into smaller containers or leave it in the bucket. Stir it lightly each time you are ready to wash clothes. Use a half-cup of this detergent per load. It does not produce a lot of suds, but don't worry about that.

Remember to try this detergent on a small load to be sure it's effective and doesn't damage your washer or clothing before you start using it heavily. If your laundry tends to be especially dirty, double the amounts of washing soda and borax to pump up the cleaning power.

## GENERAL LAUNDRY TIPS

*Wash warm, rinse cold.* The U.S. Department of Energy says that about 90% of the energy expended on washing clothes is used to heat the water. But if you wash clothes in warm water and rinse them in cold, you can cut each load's energy use in half, according to the DOE. Use hot water only for the dirtiest clothes.

*Full loads.* It's only logical, but let me just say that you use resources most efficiently when you wait until you have a full load to wash your clothes. Newer washing machines do have half-load settings, but running them twice for two smaller piles of laundry is still not as efficient as one larger load.

*Delicates and the express.* You may have some clothes made of fabric that needs to be washed separately from heavier clothes—your so-called delicates. Or maybe you need what my wife likes to call an "express"—a garment that you want to wear before you have a full load to clean with it. In these situations, you can wash them by hand in your sink or, for a slightly larger load, the bathtub. When you wash this way, soak the clothes in warm water with just a little detergent (because getting the soap out of the clothes is the only challenging part of the process, so it's better to use less than more) for about five minutes. Swirl them around in the water using your hands or the handle of a mop or plunger to help loosen any dirt. Drain the water out and gently twist the clothes to wring out the water. Rinse with cold water, and then wring the clothes again thoroughly. Hang to dry.

You can also find small, hand-cranked washers designed specifically for apartment dwellers, campers, singles, and others who live without laundry machines. These devices use even less water than hand-washing. See the Resources section on page 253 for where to find them.

*Air them out.* If your clothes haven't become stained or noticeably dirty, maybe they don't need to be washed at all, especially jeans, sweatshirts, and other layers you wear on top of other clothes. Hang them outside, and the fresh air will make them smell clean again.

*Solar clothes dryer.* Rather than sucking up energy drying your clothes with a gas or electric appliance, use the power of the sun. Set up a clothesline, and you save energy and expense, and your laundry will smell like a warm breeze on a spring day. Better yet, using a laundry line rather than a dryer helps extend the life of your clothes because the high heat inside the dryer accelerates the deterioration of many fabrics, including cotton and Lycra.

*On the line.* You can buy the classic "umbrella" type clothesline, which fits into just about any size yard and can be folded up and put away when you're having guests over. Or you can build your own laundry line with a few inexpensive materials and the most meager of construction skills. You have two choices for your clothesline: the classic "T" or a pulley system.

Whichever system you go with, try to site your clothesline on the east side of your home, so that it gets sun exposure early in the day, especially in fall and winter when the sun fades in the afternoon. Set it where air circulation is not blocked by the house, a fence, trees, a hedge, or anything else.

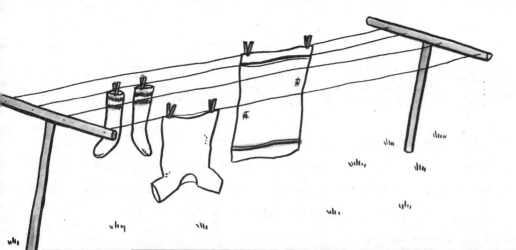

# T-BAR CLOTHESLINE

**1.** You need two 6 x 6 wooden posts and one 4 x 8 for the cross bars. Most people use treated wood for this because it stands up through many years of getting wet, but since the wood treatment is generally made from chemicals I don't like to put my hands on, I recommend naturally rot-resistant cedar, which I know is pricey. (If you choose treated wood, handle it with gloves on.) Also get a bag of quick-setting cement, eight stainless-steel eye screws, wood screws, and at least sixty feet of nylon rope. (Cotton line sags when it gets wet.)

**2.** Dig two postholes no fewer than eight feet apart and no more than twelve feet apart. The holes should be ten to twelve inches deep.

**3.** Place the posts in the holes and cement them in place.

**4.** Cut the 4 x 8 in half. Turn four of the eye screws into one side of each piece, equal distance apart.

**5.** Centering each piece on top of a post, attach it securely to the post with the wood screws.

**6.** Cut the rope into four lengths and tie each end securely to an eye screw.

**7.** When you're sure the cement is fully dry, hang your first load to dry. After you've used the line about ten times, retighten the lines by wrapping a loop or two around the eye screws.

# PULLEY CLOTHESLINE

**1.** To make a pulley line, start by identifying two sturdy spots to attach the ends, such as a corner of your house and a fence post or large tree.

**2.** Get two large stainless-steel eye screws, a pair of pulleys, a rope tightener, and nylon rope. These items are all available at home centers and hardware stores. The rope must be twice the distance plus one foot between where you've chosen to place the ends.

**3.** Drill small starter holes for each eye screw and then turn them in so that they are seated securely.

**4.** Clip the pulleys to the eye screws.

**5.** Holding both ends of the rope, thread it through one pulley and then the other. Don't worry about keeping the rope taut—you'll handle that in the next step.

**6.** Thread one end of the line into the rope tightener and tie the other end securely to the open loop at the opposite end of the rope tightener.

**7.** Pull the rope taut and trim off any excess rope, leaving three to four inches for you to grip when you pull it tight again after using it a few times.

**8.** Hang your first load to dry.

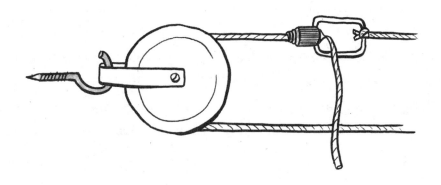

In our house we've found that most clothes and sheets come off the line soft, but towels and washcloths can sometimes be a bit stiff. Shake each of them vigorously when you take them down, and they, too, will feel fluffy and ready to dry even the tenderest skin.

## HOMEMADE SOAP

Making your own soap is an advanced homesteading challenge that's not any harder than baking, but does demand attention to safety because you work with a powerful chemical—lye, also known as sodium hydroxide, which you can buy at drugstores and online. You need to work on a clean, dry surface where the lye won't damage anything, and you should wear long sleeves, rubber cleaning gloves, and safety glasses. Lye is highly alkaline and causes a painful burning sensation on skin, so don't think you'll just protect yourself by being careful with it. Like baking, soapmaking requires you to be certain your measurements are always exact or you won't get the desired results. Also, when working with the lye, take care not to breathe the vapors or lean over the pan. Keep kids and pets away from your work area.

Here's a basic recipe:

**1.** Pour three cups of very cold water into a two-quart glass or ceramic container. Don't use a metal container—lye reacts with it.

**2.** Slowly and carefully add twelve ounces of lye, stirring as you go. This mixture gets hotter without you applying any flame or other heat to it.

**3.** Once it is mixed thoroughly, leave this solution to cool for an hour or more, until it is about 110°F.

**4.** While that is cooling, heat up 48 ounces of olive oil to the same temperature—110°F.

**5.** Carefully—at all costs, avoid splashing the

lye mixture—blend the two liquids together.

**6.** Pour the combined liquids into a 10 x 12 inch glass or plastic container lined with wax paper. (If you can't find a container that size, you can substitute a cardboard box lid, like the kind that a ream of printer paper comes in, also lined with wax paper.)

**7.** Let sit until it is consistently hard, which may take up to a week.

**8.** When the soap has hardened, cut it into blocks and wrap each with wax paper.

Once you have this basic formula working, you can start to personalize it. You can substitute or mix and match with other oils, such as coconut, almond, or hemp, or use lard or beef tallow (like the original homesteaders did) instead of the olive oil. You can also use milk—goat's milk is a popular choice because it is high in emollients that leave your skin very soft and smooth. Be sure, though, to check for the right lye concentration to use with different fats. It varies and if your lye solution isn't right, the soap will not harden. You can find online "lye calculators" (like the one at www.soapcalc.net) for just about any fat that is suitable to soap making.

You also can add essential oils to make the soap more fragrant. Lavender, vanilla, and lemon make for very pleasant scents and each has unique properties for different types of skin.

## ENERGY USE

Think of wood as stored solar energy that the tree collected and you release when you burn it. It also seems somehow to have a warming energy when you split and stack it. If you have a fireplace or, even better, a wood stove, you want it to give you the most heat as efficiently as possible. That starts with the wood.

The first and by far the most important consideration when selecting wood to burn is seasoning, or the amount of time that has passed since it was split. No matter what kind of wood you get, the logs need at least a year after they are split to dry out enough to burn well. Green, or unseasoned, wood is hard to get lit, doesn't burn thoroughly, and leaves behind a residue called "creosote" that produces noxious fumes and may even cause a fire in your chimney. Wood that is more than five years old, however, tends to be much too dry to produce much heat.

To be sure you have truly seasoned wood, you need to get it this year to use next. Whether you buy it or cut it yourself, you can tell seasoned wood because it looks dark or gray (though it's white inside when you split it) and the bark separates easily from the heartwood.

Madrone, a tree that grows in the Pacific Northwest, is said to be the best firewood because it's very dense, producing a steady high heat. But if you don't live in the madrone's range, oak, which grows everywhere, is a dense, slow, hot-burning hardwood. Hickory and birch are, too. Softwoods, such as fir and pine, don't produce quite as much heat, but they dry out and catch flame faster than hardwoods. Build your fires with both types of wood, and you will be able to start it quickly and keep it burning for hours.

Wood typically is sold in "cords," which when stacked should be four feet high, four feet wide, and eight feet long, or about 128 cubic feet of wood. You pay less for unsplit wood. You can rent a log splitter for a day at home centers, if splitting with an ax is not for you. Be sure to store your firewood off the ground (on discarded pallets) and, if you can, under a roof rather than a plastic tarp, which traps condensation and slows the seasoning process.

To build a long-lasting, safe, and warm fire, start by placing a large, heavy log on the back of the grate (parallel to the back of the fireplace) and a medium-size log in the front of the grate, leaving at least two to three inches between them. (Actually, the real first step is to open the flue, so I hope this is just a reminder.) Roll six to eight sheets of newspaper or other scrap paper into tubes and stuff them between, under, and around the logs. Lay a half-dozen or so dry twigs and/or pieces of bark across (perpendicular to) the logs. My father-in-law, a great fire-builder, taught me to hold one rolled-up paper in my hand and light it first to start creating an updraft and then use it to light the other paper at both ends and, if possible, in the center. I realize this isn't the safest practice, but if done with care, it does help get the smoke the paper will produce heading up the chimney rather than back into the room.

As the paper turns to ash, look to see if the kindling (twigs and bark) has caught fire. If not, add a few more sheets of paper. When the kindling is burning, add two small logs in the same direction as the kindling. When the logs are half to two-thirds burnt, add more, two at a time, building the pile up in a cross-hatched pattern. Always be sure to leave space between logs to allow air to flow through—fires need oxygen as much as they need wood. Flames do emit heat, but your fire really begins warming the room when some of the wood turns to glowing orange coals.

## MORE ENERGY EFFICIENCY

Even without a fireplace or wood stove, you can reduce your need for fossil fuels to heat—and cool—your home. A row of shrubs or evergreen trees planted on the north and east side of your home deflects cold winter winds and reduces your heating costs. Tall, leafy trees and shrubs on the south and west side of your house provide shade that keeps your home cooler on hot days. Even planting a small tree that shades your air-conditioning unit can increase its efficiency by as much as 10%, according to the U.S. Department of Energy.

You can reduce your energy demand with a few simple measures you take inside, too. Keep a solid layer of insulation in the attic, garage, or anywhere else walls are exposed to the outside. Be sure your windows and doors are as airtight as possible. Seal cracks around window casements and doors with caulk. Also, don't allow furniture, drapes, or anything else to block vents. Drapes add extra insulation for your windows. Close curtains during hot days to keep your house cooler, open them on sunny days in winter to let the sunshine help warm it.

## Pest Control

**Insects in your garden are inevit-**able, and essential. In your home they are nearly as inevitable, even if they're not essential. Or maybe they are and we aren't, but I understand that you don't want bugs crawling all over your home. But that's no reason to schedule a monthly visit from an exterminator, nor is it necessary to buy spray cans full of chemicals that are poisonous to just about every living thing, particularly you, your family, and your pets. Instead, I'll share with you some safe, effective solutions that you can rely on to curb an insect invasion.

Before you try any solution, though, take the time to figure out why the bugs are in your house. You can kill all the bugs you see, but until you deal with the conditions that entice them into your home, they will keep coming back. Access to food is one of the primary reasons bugs come into your house. It sounds obvious, but don't leave food (or even crumbs) on your floors, counters, sink, or any place else. Pet food may attract insects and rodents—be sure to put away your animal's bowl when feeding time is over. You probably know that moths feed on wool and other fabrics. They also may subsist on hair and lint they find on floors and carpets, if you don't sweep or vacuum regularly. Termites and carpenter ants seek out weak or rotted wood. Many pests may also come inside your house in search of water they can find from a drippy faucet or a tiny leak they find. The more you keep your home clean and well maintained, the more likely it is that the pests will leave you be.

Before we move on to active pest controls you can use, please indulge me in a few words in defense of spiders. I know they creep many people out; my teenage son can't even tolerate a toy spider near him. But remember this: spiders prey on many of the most bothersome pests, including flies, moths, and fleas. And with only a couple rare exceptions, spiders do not bite people. (The exceptions are black widow and brown recluse spiders, which are rarely found in homes and do not live at all in many regions of North America.) So if you see spiderwebs in your house, by all means sweep or vacuum them up, but leave the spiders to continue eliminating other pests for you.

## ANTS

With the exception of fire ants, whose bites are very painful, ants are generally beneficial insects outside, where they function as the ecosystem's garbage removal team. To get rid of fire ants and other types of ants that have become a nuisance outside, pour boiling water on their nest. It may take a few applications to fully kill the colony, but the treatment will work.

Inside, they can be bothersome, though not really a threat of any kind. They're easy to eliminate using this simple trap and bait.

**1.** Start by making the bait. Thoroughly dissolve one teaspoon of boric acid (available at drugstores and supermarkets) and six tablespoons of sugar in two cups of water. Use a clear jar so you can see when all the boric acid crystals are dissolved.

**2.** Using old plastic containers with lids, like margarine or soft cream cheese cartons, punch several holes in the sides of the tubs, near the bottom so the ants can get inside.

**3.** Soak cotton balls in the bait solution, put them into the containers, and cover them with lids so the bait doesn't evaporate.

**4.** Place the bait containers wherever you see ant trails, in or outside the house.

**5.** Watch and wait. This trap is most effective when the worker ants continually carry low doses of boric acid back to feed the other ants in the nest. Boric acid is mildly repellent to ants, so mixing a very low dose with sugar makes it more likely that surviving ants will continue eating the bait and taking it back to the nest.

**6.** Clean the containers and use fresh bait solution at least once a week.

## COCKROACHES

Few pests provoke disgust and loathing like cockroaches do, and if you live in an apartment building where other tenants leave food and garbage accessible to them, they can be hard to get rid of. You can poison them using the same boric acid trap I recommended for ants, though you need to double or even triple the concentration of the borax in the bait to make it effective against roaches. You will still see roaches for three or four of days after you set the trap out as they slowly carry the mildly poisonous bait back to their colony. If you are not seeing their numbers diminish after a few days, increase the borax concentration. (The reason you don't want to make the solution too strong is that you don't want to deter them from taking the sugary bait back to their colony to feed others.)

The challenge of getting rid of cockroaches is that they may continue to come into your home from other apartments where residents are not as diligent about cleaning up. In that case, you want to see if you can discover where the roaches are coming into your apartment or their pathways after they are in. Once you have figured that out, you can spread diatomaceous earth around the entryway. It is a naturally occurring mineral (fossilized plants) with sharp edges that wound the roaches when they walk through it. Clean up the dead bugs and refresh the layer of DE every week or two. You can find DE at many garden centers and online—just be sure to get the kind for pest control, not the type that is used in swimming pool filters, which won't be effective because it is ground up differently and doesn't have the same sharp edges you want for gashing open roaches.

## FLIES

The fly family has thousands of different members, and the ones that find their way into your house are rarely more than simply annoying. (Many of those you see in your garden are quite beneficial because their larvae parasitize pests such as caterpillars.) Flies do the important work of consuming waste, so the best way to keep them from overrunning your home is not to leave rotting food and garbage accessible to them. This can be a challenge if you keep a compost bucket in your kitchen, as we do. Make sure it has a secure lid and empty it at least every two or three days.

Using pesticides to control flies is a bit like using a bazooka to shoot a squirrel—yes, it will do the job, but there's sure to be a lot of unnecessary collateral damage. Fly swatters are a more appropriate weapon for the job. An even better option

that is less taxing on your attention and reflexes is a trap. I don't mean a Venus flytrap, a plant that eats pests, which are very effective. I'm referring to a trap that flies stick to or lures them in with bait and then prevents them from getting out. You can buy traps like those—be sure to get one that is not treated with pesticides—or you can make them yourself.

Squirt a thin bead of honey or maple syrup down the middle of a strip of duct tape (the sticky side), and you have a very basic flytrap. When the flies land on it to eat the sweetener, their feet get stuck. Hang a couple of these near your garbage cans or wherever you see flies congregating, and before long they'll be encrusted with flies.

Construct a bottle trap from an empty two-liter soda bottle. About two-thirds up from the bottom of the bottle, cut off the top portion. Remove the cap and turn the top part upside down, and tape or glue it securely to the bottom half. If you want to hang the trap when you're finished, punch holes on either side through both sections on opposite sides of the bottle, and loop a length of string through the holes. Fill the bottom section with water and a few squirts of liquid dish soap. Bait the trap by spreading a bit of jelly around the edge of the top where the cap goes. The flies come in to get the jelly, and few if any of them will be able to get out. You'll see them floating in the water.

## MOSQUITOES

Few things ruin a nice late summer evening sitting on your patio or balcony as surely as mosquitoes do. Their bites are mildly painful and itchy, and very aggravating. And now many people fear mosquito bites because they can spread potentially lethal West Nile Virus. The solution for many people who don't want to run inside has been to slather on chemical insect repellent. DEET (known to chemists as N,N-Diethyl-meta-toluamide) is the active ingredient in most commercial insect repellents, and when applied repeatedly to the skin, it has been known to cause rashes, headaches, restlessness, and irritability, particularly in young children.

An alternative that appeals to many homeowners are "bug-zappers," which purportedly lure pests to their blue lights and then electrocute them when they get close. Despite what the advertisements claim, these devices do not control mosquitoes because the pests are not attracted to light. (This is a great solution for killing moths, which are attracted to light; but moths are hardly pests outside, and they can be very beautiful.) Mosquitoes are lured in by carbon dioxide, the gas you and all other mammals exhale with every breath. The little biters are most active at dusk—the time of day when we are most likely to be relaxing outside. You can find mosquito traps with carbon dioxide lures (and powered by electricity or propane) selling for up to $1,500, but independent research shows they are not very effective at reducing mosquito populations.

Your first line of defense against mosquitoes in your yard is to get rid of standing water, where mosquitoes lay their eggs. Even a small puddle that lingers for more than three days is likely to become a breeding ground for mosquitoes in summer. You also want to recruit the food chain to help control the mosquito population. Bats eat thousands of mosquitoes each night, and they come out to feed at exactly the same time the pests get busy snacking on you. If you don't have a bat colony around your home, you can buy or build a very simple bat house, hang it high in a tree, and before long you'll see them as it begins to get dark each night flapping and swooping around, gobbling up mosquitoes. Purple martins are members of the swallow family that also feed on mosquitoes, which is why many farmers set up houses for them near ponds and watering holes. Purple martin houses can be expensive, but they also make an attractive addition to your landscape—though not a fraction as beautiful as the inhabitants.

You can protect yourself from mosquitoes the natural way by growing citrus-scented herbs such as lemongrass and lemon balm. Before you sit down outside, break off a few stems and leaves from the herbs, crush them gently in your hands, and rub them on all your exposed skin. I'm not going to promise this will give you 100% deterrence for hours on end, but I've found I rarely get bit while coated with these essential oils. And I think I smell nice, too.

## STINKBUGS AND OTHER OCCASIONAL PESTS

Asian stinkbugs are relative newcomers to our continent that are quickly making real nuisances of themselves. Because they are an alien species, they don't yet have natural predators here to keep them in check. So far, they've been found clustering in houses on the East Coast, but scientists tracking them have observed that they are rapidly expanding their territory. If you squish them by hand or foot, you will not fail to notice the very pungent sulfury stink they emit.

Ladybugs are very beneficial insects in your garden (their larvae eat pests like aphids), but in cold climates they come inside houses and gather in large clusters.

Crickets, beetles, and other insects also may find their way into your home, where you don't want them.

When you need to get rid of any of these bugs, don't reach for the can of poison. Grab your handheld vacuum cleaner instead. Hit the power button to High and suck up the little buggers, then dump them outside where they'll become food for other creatures.

## YELLOW JACKETS AND OTHERS WASPS

Wasp and hornet larvae prey on garden pests, but none of us ever wants to see them in their adult stage. They sting painfully and often. Yellow jackets are especially a pest at late summer cookouts. You can use the same homemade trap I described for catching flies (page 215) to lure many of them away from where they can bother you and trap them there. Hang the trap about 15 feet away from your food table.

# Home Remedies

**I'm not a doctor—and I've never** played one on TV. I'm not a trained herbalist, and I don't claim to be a healer of any kind. But just as you can control pests and solve many other minor household problems without buying products at the store, I have found that you can treat minor ailments with remedies made from plants in and around your garden. Now, before I share a few of the herbal remedies I've found easiest to use and most reliable, let me give the all-important caveat:

Information you read here is not intended to be a substitute for professional medical care. Always check with your physician or other qualified health provider about any serious medical condition. You assume all risk (and hold me and the publisher of this book completely blameless) for using any of the information found here. Got it?

## ALOE

The easy-to-grow houseplant known as aloe vera has thick stems that ooze a pale green gel when they're broken open. Many herbal medicine experts say that the gel has antibacterial, anti-inflammatory, and antiviral properties. It has proven most handy around our house for soothing minor burns, including sunburn, and treating small cuts and abrasions. You can use it just by breaking off one of the stems and squeezing out the gel onto the affected area. As with all of these remedies, use only a little at first to be sure you don't have a strong negative reaction to it.

## CHAMOMILE

A pretty member of the daisy family, chamomile tea has long been used to soothe stomach distress and help people relax before bedtime. If you remember the classic children's story *The Tale of Peter Rabbit*, the mother bunny gave her son a cup of chamomile tea when he came home from his afternoon munching away in Farmer McGregor's garden. My great-aunt was quick to brew a cup of chamomile tea whenever she heard my siblings or me pass gas.

## GARLIC

You can protect yourself from colds just by eating great-tasting food. Seriously, research has shown that people who eat garlic frequently catch fewer colds, and when they do get a cold, the symptoms are less severe. Garlic also is linked to reduce risk of heart disease, cancer, and many other health benefits. It has a clearly established connection to the best-tasting marinara sauce, stir-fry, and crusty Italian bread.

## JEWELWEED

You probably haven't intentionally planted jewelweed, but if you have had an encounter with poison ivy (in your yard or walking in the woods), the orange-flowered plant is likely to be growing not too far away—they seem to thrive in the same conditions. Which is very convenient, because the sap from jewelweed's stems can protect you from the rash caused by poison ivy and can reduce its duration if you do get the oil from poison ivy on your skin. If you can, apply the sap before you go near poison ivy to create a barrier. Some people report that jewelweed sap also helps speed the healing of mosquito bites and bee stings, too.

## LAVENDER

When choosing herbs for your garden, lavender should be near the top of your list. It is beautiful, sporting stalks of pink to purple flowers in the height of summer, very drought-resistant and nearly care-free. Most of all, lavender is delightfully fragrant—you'll catch a whiff every time you brush by it, which becomes almost irresistible once you discover that. Something about that fragrance seems to soothe stress and calm nerves. Research has confirmed what folklore has long claimed—lavender flowers in your bath-water or crushed inside a pillow promote relaxation and ease anxiety. The University of Maryland's complementary medicine department also reports on research that found people suffering dramatic hair loss slowed or even reversed that process by massaging their scalps with the essential oil from lavender. I can't attest to that personally, but if you or someone you are affected, adding a few drops of lavender oil to your shampoo certainly couldn't hurt.

## MINT

The leaves from homegrown mint make a tasty tea—hot or iced—that calms your stomach when you've overeaten or just feel queasy. Peppermint works best, I've found, but almost any kind of mint works. Making the tea couldn't be easier—just drop a handful of fresh leaves into boiling water, and let it steep until the water turns a pale yellow-green.

# A TO Z
# GROWING GUIDE

**T**o help you get started producing some of your own food, I've compiled the basic information you need to plant and care for fifty-four vegetables and herbs, with hints on the best choices for small gardens and containers.

# A

## ARUGULA

*What to plant:* Seeds. Italian seed companies offer different varieties, but to me they all seem to grow and taste the same.

*When to plant:* As soon as you can work the soil in spring, and in late summer, when night temperatures drop below 70°F.

*Planting and growing tips:*
- A fast-growing crop, arugula is ready to snip off leaves for eating thirty to forty days after you plant the seeds.
- Arugula's flavor gets spicier as the leaves grow larger.
- When temperatures warm up in spring, arugula grows flower stalks and then blooms. Time to pull it and replace with a hot weather crop. You can eat arugula's peppery yellow flowers, if you like.
- Where winter is not too frigid, you can plant arugula in fall and cover it with mulch after it sprouts. It survives winter and starts growing again in the spring.

## ASPARAGUS

*What to plant:* Crowns, or one-year-old root clusters. All-male varieties such as Jersey Giant, Jersey Prince, and Jersey Knight, are more productive than old-fashioned types, which include lower-yielding females.

*When to plant:* When your garden's soil temperature is warmer than 50°F.

*Planting and growing tips:*
- Asparagus needs three years before you can begin harvesting but it can continue producing for fifteen years after that. Choose a spot for it where you won't be digging and planting other crops.
- Dig a trench six to eight inches deep. Add compost and form small mounds eight to ten inches apart. Place one asparagus crown on top of each mound and gently spread out the roots. Backfill with the soil you dug out up to the level where the top of the crown is at the soil line. Gradually backfill with the rest of the soil as the plant grows.
- Do not harvest any spears the first two

seasons or you will diminish the yields in future years. In the third year, take a few of the largest spears. After that, harvest all spears that are thicker than a pencil.

- When the harvest ends, asparagus grows large ferny leaves. Leave them on the plant through fall and winter, then trim them to the ground in spring.

# B

## BASIL

*What to plant:* Seeds or plants. Sweet or Genovese varieties are the common choice for pesto or Caprese salad, but you have many other choices, including Thai and Cuban, which have smaller leaves and a spicier flavor.

*When to plant:* A week or so after the last frost in spring. Basil doesn't tolerate cold.

*Planting and growing tips:*
- If your growing season is short or if you are new to growing basil, start with plants rather than seeds.

- Once your basil plants start to branch out, start trimming off the top. Clip off the top third of the plants two or three times—about two weeks apart—and they will grow bushier and produce more leaves.

- You can trim off and eat leaves as needed, making sure a few leaves are left behind on each stem. In about a week, you'll see new growth again.

## BEANS

*What to plant:* Seeds. Pole types need to be staked, but they take up less space than the bush varieties. Kentucky Wonder and Blue Lake bear lots of straight, juicy pods. Dried beans come in dozens of varieties, including kidney beans, chickpeas, lentils and black turtle beans.

*When to plant:* Spring, after the last frost. Where the first frost doesn't come until October, you can also plant green beans in late summer for fall harvest.

*Planting and growing tips:*
- Beans, like other members of the legume family, pull nitrogen (a key nutrient) from

the air so you don't need to fertilize them.

- Use stakes that are six to seven feet tall for pole beans. Any taller and you may not be able to reach the uppermost beans; on shorter stakes, the bean vines get tangled.
- Avoid working in the bean patch when it is wet (even from dew). You risk spreading fungal diseases from one plant to the next.
- Once the plants start producing beans, pick them every day or at least every other. Smaller beans are tenderer, and the plant will continue to pop out new ones to replace the ones you picked.
- Leave dried bean pods on the vine until they begin to turn brown.

## BEETS

*What to plant:* Seeds. You can go with a classic red variety, such as Detroit Dark Red, or try a red-and-white striped or golden type. Bull's Blood has striking dark red leaves and deep red roots.

*When to plant:* About four weeks before the last frost in spring.

*Planting and growing tips:*

- Beets need loose soil with as few rocks as possible to form smooth, evenly shaped roots.
- When you plant beet seeds too close together—and in my experience, it's almost impossible to avoid—you have to pull out the extras so that there are five inches or more between them. Eat the thinnings in a salad or any way that you would eat spinach.
- The roots are most tender and flavorful when they just start to show through the soil line. They get woodier and drier as they grow larger.
- If you are succession planting (see page 17), follow beets with tomatoes or a member of the squash family.

# BROCCOLI

*What to plant:* Seedlings. Calabrese is a popular heirloom, Green Comet is valued for the many extra side shoots it produces. Or get all adventurous with a purple broccoli or even a romanesco.

*When to plant:* Spring or late summer, when overnight temperatures are warmer than 50°F and daytime temperatures are cooler than 80°F.

*Planting and growing tips:*
- The first few days after you transplant the seedlings are critical for their survival. They tolerate cold, but they need to be kept constantly moist until they start to grow again.
- When you harvest a head of broccoli, leave some of the main stalk in the garden. Fertilize it with compost tea or other liquid organic fertilizer and in a few weeks small broccoli heads will form on the sides of the remaining stalk.
- Caterpillars are broccoli's number one pest. Row covers (a fabric that lets light, air and water in, while keeping moths out) are the best way to avoid biting into a caterpillar.

# BRUSSELS SPROUTS

*What to plant:* Seedlings. Long Island Improved, an heirloom, is disease-resistant. Jade Cross is more productive, Oliver is quicker to ripen. Rubine has reddish stalks and sprouts.

*When to plant:* Mid to late summer—about six weeks before your area's average first frost in fall.

*Planting and growing tips:*
- To get the biggest, healthiest plants, leave eighteen inches or more between the seedlings.
- When the nights get colder than 45°F, clip off the stalk's growing point to concentrate the plant's energy on filling out the existing sprouts.
- Harvest the whole stalk or some of the sprouts, whichever suits you. Either way, wait for a couple of light frosts to sweeten the sprouts' flavor before you pick them.

- A stalk-full of sprouts will keep in a garage or other cool spot for a few weeks after harvest.

# C

## CABBAGE

*What to plant:* Seeds or seedlings. Choose a variety based on what you want it for—eating fresh, cooking, or sauerkraut. The longer the variety's maturation time, the better it is for cooking or storing. Green and red types, along with bok choy and other Asian cabbages, have similar needs and habits.

*When to plant:* Early spring for harvesting in summer or midsummer for a fall crop.

*Planting and growing tips:*
- Cabbage grows best where it gets a little shade during the day.
- Leave at least a foot between each cabbage plant so that the heads have enough room to reach full size.
- Constant, even moisture is crucial for heavy, solid heads. Keep a few inches of organic mulch around cabbage at all times to prevent the soil from drying out.

## CARROTS

*What to plant:* Seeds. The familiar long-rooted Nantes and Danvers are best in loose soil. In the heaviest soil, go with a shorter, stumpier type like Thumbelina. You aren't limited to orange—heirloom seed companies are offering purple, red, yellow, and white varieties.

*When to plant:* As soon as the soil is dry and not too cold to dig in spring.

*Planting and growing tips:*
- The looser the soil, the better the carrots will grow. Add lots of compost to loosen dense, clay soils.
- After sowing the seeds, cover them lightly with soil or, even better, fine compost. Be sure you don't pat the soil down so hard the tiny seeds can't break through when they sprout.
- When the carrots poke up above ground, mound up soil or mulch to cover them

and prevent the sun from turning them green.

- You can leave carrots in the ground until you're ready to eat them. Surround them with several inches of straw, shredded leaves or other organic mulch so the soil stays pliable enough for you to get the carrots out when the temperatures are freezing.

## CANTALOUPES AND OTHER MUSKMELONS

*What to plant:* Seeds (where summers are long and hot) or seedlings (everywhere else). Cantaloupes are an orange-fleshed, netted muskmelon. Other varieties may have smooth skin or green flesh, and slightly different flavors.

*When to plant:* A week or two after the last frost date in spring. This is a warm weather crop.

*Planting and growing tips:*
- Covering the soil in spring with black plastic mulch helps warm it enough to grow muskmelons in the North.
- Plant muskmelons in clusters of four and leave enough room around each cluster for the vines to spread three feet or more in all directions. If you don't have enough room for that, grow the vines on a trellis and help support the fruit as it gets heavy in a "hammock" made from T-shirts, panty hose or any other stretchable fabric.
- Muskmelons are ripe and ready to harvest when the area where the vines connect to the fruit turns brown.

## CAULIFLOWER

*What to plant:* Seedlings. Snow Crown, Snow King, and Snowball all have their partisans, though there do not seem to be meaningful differences among them. So-called self-blanching types often still need a little help from you to be sure they completely cover the head.

*When to plant:* Early to midsummer. Cauliflower needs consistently cool temperatures—fall-like—as it matures.

- To form full, substantial heads, cauliflower needs fertile soil with a complete set of nutrients. Mix lots of compost into the soil before planting.
- About three weeks after planting cauliflower, scratch an inch-deep layer of compost (or aged manure) into the soil around the plants.
- Direct sunlight turns cauliflower heads green and bitter. When the head is still smaller than your fist, gently pull the large leaves up over the head and tie them in place with twine. Be sure the leaves and head are dry when you do this to prevent trapping moisture and causing the head to rot.
- Feel the head inside the leaves with your hands. When it feels full, the head is ready for harvest.

## CHARD

*What to plant:* Seeds. The traditional white varieties, such as Fordhook Giant, are more productive but not as attractive as newer types like Bright Lights, which have red, yellow and orange stems.

*When to plant:* Right after the last frost date.

*Planting and growing tips:*

- Swiss chard tolerates heat better than spinach, but as the temperatures warm it grows taller, leafier and less tender. A little shade in summer slows this process.
- You won't plant an easier to grow, more trouble-free crop than Swiss chard.
- Harvest leaves only as you need them and the plant will continue to make new ones until frost.

## CHERVIL

*What to plant:* Seeds, or seedlings (if spring quickly becomes hot where you live). The plain and curly types taste and smell very much alike.

*When to plant:* Late winter/early spring or late summer.

*Planting and growing tips:*

- Like just about every herb, chervil suffers in soggy spots. Plant it where the soil drains quickly after a storm.

- Chervil's tiny white flowers attract the beneficial insects that prey on pests. Plant it in and among your vegetable crops to help protect them from infestations.
- You can start harvesting the feathery leaves about six weeks after you plant the seeds.

## CHIVES

*What to plant:* Seedlings. Beware of garlic chives—they spread rampantly and soon invade every bed in your garden.

*When to plant:* Early spring is usual, but you can plant them at any time during the growing season.

*Planting and growing tips:*
- Chives are perennial, meaning you plant them once and they grow back every year. Put them in a spot where you won't disturb them.
- In late spring, chives blooms with puffy purple flowers you can eat or just cut off.
- Cut chives as you want to eat them, and at the end of the growing season, trim them down to a few inches high.

- Dig up and divide clumps of chives every three to five years. You can share the new clumps with friends or pot them up and bring them inside to grow on a windowsill.

## CILANTRO

*What to plant:* Seeds. "Slow-bolt" varieties are best for areas where spring heats up quickly.

*When to plant:* Three to four weeks before the last frost in spring.

*Planting and growing tips:*
- Cilantro flowers attract bees and other pollinators. Plant it around your vegetable beds to help boost your yields of other crops.
- Cilantro bolts, or flowers and starts producing seeds, when the soil gets warmer than 70°F. Pull it and replace it with a hot weather crop in summer, or let it go to seed. The seeds will drop and come up the following spring.
- The pods that form after the flowers finish blooming are filled with seeds that

are the spice known as coriander. You can gather some of them to dry and use in your kitchen.

## COLLARDS

*What to plant:* Seeds. Georgia Green, an heirloom, produces large heads and tolerates heat. Champion is more compact, so it fits into smaller spaces, and it's more winter-hardy than most varieties.

*When to plant:* Midsummer, about three months before the first frost in fall.

*Planting and growing tips:*
- Deep-rooted collards grow best in loose soil. Dig and fluff the soil eight inches deep or more. Mix in nitrogen-rich materials like well-rotted manure.
- Collards sprout in soil as cold as 45°F and as warm as 75°F. In warm soil, the seedlings will come up in as little as a week; they may take up to three weeks in cooler conditions.
- For best flavor, wait until after a light frost or two before harvesting. Snip off and eat the lower and outer leaves and the plant

will continue producing new ones.

## CORN

*What to plant:* Seeds. Heirlooms like Country Gentleman have the true "corny" flavor. Newer hybrids, such as Silver Queen and How Sweet It Is, have been bred for extra sweetness. Popcorn needs a long growing season before it's ready to harvest.

*When to plant:* A week or two after the last frost date.

*Planting and growing tips:*
- Corn seeds do not germinate in cold, damp soil. Wait until the overnight air temperatures are warmer than 60°F and the ground has dried out before planting them.
- Cross-pollination happens readily among different corn varieties. Plant only one at a time to avoid harvesting ears that have all sorts of weird variations.
- A heavy feeder, corn needs a lot of nitrogen at the start of its growing cycle. Mix in composted (not fresh!) poultry manure

or other high-nitrogen organic fertilizer into the soil a few weeks before planting.

- Nourish corn with compost tea or other liquid organic fertilizer every other week from the time the seedlings first poke up through the soil until the ears start to form.
- Thwart a corn earworm infestation with a few drops of vegetable or mineral oil in the tip of each ear.
- Corn is ready to harvest when the silk has turned brown and a milky fluid squirts out of the kernels when pressed with your fingernail.

## CUCUMBERS

*What to plant:* Seeds in warm climates, seedlings where the growing season is short. If you plan to grow them up a trellis, look for vining rather than bush varieties. Smaller pickling types grow on the shortest vines.

*When to plant:* Two weeks after the last frost in spring.

*Planting and growing tips:*

- Cucumber varieties typically have both male and female flowers. The males open first and produce pollen, but no fruit. Some newer varieties produce mostly or only female flowers. Seed packs of these varieties include a few seeds (usually marked with dye) of a variety with male flowers to pollinate the females. You need to take care of the male or you will have lots of female flowers and no cucumbers.
- Save space by guiding cucumber vines to grow on a structure, such as a trellis. This is also increases air circulation, preventing fungal diseases that plague cucumbers, and it keeps the fruit away from ground-dwelling pests.
- When cucumbers don't get steady moisture, the flavor can turn bitter.
- Don't plant cucumbers where you last grew squash or melons—they are closely related and some diseases that afflict all of them live in the soil.

## D ▰▰▰▰▰▰▰▰▰▰▰▰▰▰▰

### DILL

*What to plant:* Seeds. Dukat produces tasty seeds and tender foliage. Long Island can reach up to five feet tall.

*When to plant:* Anytime after the last frost date has passed.

*Planting and growing tips:*
- Sow dill seeds only a half-inch deep and cover them lightly with soil.
- The ideal spacing is nine inches between each plant, but if your garden gets steady air flow, you can plant it much closer.
- If you let dill flower and go to seed, it replants itself in your garden—everywhere. Fortunately, the sprouts are easy to recognize and pull out where you don't want them. Dill is a biennial, which means that the seeds are produced in the plants' second growing season, so don't pull it out in fall.

## E ▰▰▰▰▰▰▰▰▰▰▰▰▰▰▰

### EGGPLANT

*What to plant:* Seedlings. Black Beauty is the classic, large, purple Italian type. Easter Egg bears white, oval-shaped fruit. Turkish Italian Orange has bright-colored fruit. Bambino produces lots of little fruit on a plant that reaches just a foot high—perfect for containers and small plots.

*When to plant:* When the soil has warmed to at least 60°F. Don't rush—eggplant is very vulnerable to cold.

*Planting and growing tips:*
- Choose a spot for your eggplant where you have not recently grown tomatoes or peppers, its cousins in the nightshade family.
- Eggplant is most productive if it gets at least eight hours of direct sun each day.
- If a cold spell occurs after you've planted eggplant, cover it at night with row cover fabric or just an old sheet.
- Use small tomato cages or stakes to hold up eggplant heavily laden with fruit.
- As eggplants grow larger, they become

tougher, seedier and more bitter. Pick them when they're no more than four inches in diameter. Frequent picking stimulates the plant to continue producing new eggplant.

# F

## FENNEL

*What to plant:* Seeds. Bronze fennel is attractive and produces lots of aromatic and tasty seeds, but a very small bulb. Florence fennel (or "finocchio") grows a large white bulb that can be braised whole or shredded for eating fresh or in cooked dishes.

*When to plant:* Early spring, as soon as you can work the soil.

*Planting and growing tips:*
- Fennel grows vigorously even in poor soil. Plant it where other crops do not fare well.
- You may have to wait as long as three weeks for fennel seeds to sprout.
- Harvest fennel seeds after the flowers turn brown by simply rubbing the dried

blossom with your hands. Do this over a bowl or other container to catch the seeds as they fall.
- If you leave a few flowers on the plant, the seeds fall and replant themselves for the next year's crop.

# G

## GARLIC

*What to plant:* Cloves from mature bulbs. Hardneck types tolerate a wide variety of conditions—this group includes red- and purple-streaked varieties. Softnecks are better suited to braiding. Do not try to grow from cloves purchased at the grocery store—they are typically treated with an anti-sprouting agent.

*When to plant:* Fall, around the time of the first frost.

*Planting and growing tips:*
- Garlic needs a chilling period to form full-size bulbs. After planting in fall, garlic grows a few leaves and then becomes dormant through the winter. It starts

growing again when the weather warms in spring.

- Weeds are tough competition for garlic. Keep them away from garlic with a solid layer of straw, shredded leaves or other organic mulch. Pull any weeds that come through it as soon as possible.
- In late spring, hardneck garlic varieties produce a "scape," or seedpod on a long stalk. When it is full and plump, cut it off and add its mild, garlicky flavor to a stir-fry or other dish.
- Garlic is ready to harvest in midsummer, after the aboveground leaves have turned brown and flopped over.
- Save a few of your best cloves to plant for your next crop.

# H ▬▬▬▬▬▬▬▬

## HORSERADISH

*What to plant:* Root cutting. You can buy a cutting from a nursery or any piece of root you can get from another gardener or at the store will grow into a new plant.

*When to plant:* Anytime you can get a chunk of root to plant and can dig in the soil.

*Planting and growing tips:*

- Horseradish is a perennial that comes back every year. Left to its own devices, horseradish spreads aggressively and will soon colonize the whole garden. To control it in a small space, plant it in a deep container, which you can bury in the ground or keep on a patio or deck.
- Dig a hole that's deep enough to stand the root cutting up in. While holding the root, backfill the hole with soil until all of the root is covered but the very top, known as the "crown."
- Horseradish needs no fertilizer or any other care. Plant it and ignore it.
- Cold temperatures improve the flavor of horseradish. Harvest it in after frost in fall or in early spring, by digging up the root. Remember, every piece of root you leave behind will grow into a new horseradish. Try to dig up the whole root and just replant a chunk or two for next year's harvest.

# K

## KALE

*What to plant:* Seeds or seedlings. Curly or savoyed (crinkly) varieties tend to be tenderer. Dwarf Green Curled is a sensible choice for containers and small spaces. Red and purplish varieties such as Red Russian are colorful enough to fit into a flowerbed.

*When to plant:* Mid to late summer, about three months before the first frost in fall (for seeds) or six weeks before the first frost (seedlings).

*Planting and growing tips:*

• Though kale is mostly trouble-free, avoid planting it where you've grown cabbage, broccoli, or other members of the cabbage family in the last three growing seasons.

• A handful or two of compost in the planting furrow or hole is all the fertilizing kale needs.

• Kale tastes best after a few frosts have sweetened its flavor. It can survive in your garden until a week or two of very cold temperatures shut down its growth and wilt its leaves.

## KOHLRABI

*What to plant:* Seeds. Grand Duke has tender bulbs. Early Purple Vienna has an attractive color and is ready to eat six weeks after planting.

*When to plant:* As soon as the daytime temperatures are consistently in the 50s in spring and in late summer for a fall crop.

*Planting and growing tips:*

• A quick spring crop, kohlrabi is an ideal choice to plant where you plan to grow tomatoes, peppers or other heat-loving crops in summer.

• A mix of purple, pale green and white kohlrabis makes an eye-catching and practical container.

• Kohlrabi is ready to harvest when the bulb is about the size of a baseball. The flavor turns bitter as it grows larger than that.

# L

## LEEKS

*What to plant:* Seedlings. The best-tasting varieties, such as American Flag and King Richard, need up to 130 days to mature (though you can harvest them earlier, as baby leeks). Blue Solaise can be planted in fall and harvested in spring.

*When to plant:* Around the last frost date in spring.

*Planting and growing tips:*
- Get leek seedlings that are more than six inches tall. Cover all but a couple inches of the stems with soil.
- As the leeks grow, mound soil or mulch around the base to keep the stem white instead of turning green. This "blanching" gives the leek a sweeter flavor.
- Leeks, like other members of the onion family, have shallow roots and do not compete well with weeds. Protect them with mulch and vigilance.

## LETTUCE

*What to plant:* Seeds and seedlings. Leaf lettuces let you mix and match shapes, textures and colors, and they give you a continuous harvest. Romaine is an easy to grow head lettuce that's more heat tolerant than most.

*When to plant:* As soon as the soil is warm and dry enough to work in spring and two weeks after that and two weeks after that. And again three times more in late summer.

*Planting and growing tips:*
- To get the longest spring harvest of lettuce, as well as mâché, mesclun, and other salad greens, plant seeds and seedlings at the same time, then follow with sowing seeds twice more at two-week intervals.
- Place lettuce where it will be shaded by taller plants, such as tomatoes, later in the season to help it last longer as the temperatures heat up.
- You can begin harvesting the leaves as soon as they are more than four inches long. Leave at least five behind to fuel

the growth of new ones.

- If you live where it is damp in the morning, look for slugs on and in your lettuce plants (their favorite food) and remove the pests before they eat your salad. Then put out the traps on page 56.
- Feed lettuce with a dose of compost tea or liquid organic fertilizer after each harvest.

# M

## MARJORAM

*What to plant:* Seedlings. Sweet marjoram has better flavor than wild or pot marjorams.

*When to plant:* Right after the last frost has passed in spring.

*Planting and growing tips:*
- Marjoram grows to about three feet tall and almost as wide, which makes it an attractive green accent plant in flowerbeds.
- It also grows well in containers, by itself or with flowers or other herbs.

- Marjoram is very drought-tolerant—plant it in the hottest, driest spot in your garden.
- Before the first frost in fall, dig up a clump or two of marjoram and pot them in small containers. Put them where they will get sunlight and you can clip fresh, fragrant leaves to season your meals all winter.

## MUSTARD

*What to plant:* Seeds or seedlings. Green Wave is more heat-tolerant than most varieties. Osaka Purple matures in as little as three weeks, stays compact, and has striking deep-red to purple veins in the green leaves.

*When to plant:* As soon as you can work the soil in spring and in late summer.

*Planting and growing tips:*
- Plant mustard where it will be shaded in late spring and early summer to extend its growing season.
- For milder flavor, keep consistently moist. Allowing the soil to dry out between

waterings makes mustard more pungent.

- When the weather turns warm, mustard flowers and then forms seedpods. The edible flowers and the seeds add a spicy flavor to raw and cooked dishes.

O ▬▬▬▬▬▬▬▬▬▬

## OKRA

*What to plant:* Seeds. Clemson Spineless, an heirloom, bears big pods without the many little prickles on most varieties. Burgundy's stems, leaves and pods have vivid red highlights. Early maturing Jade is best for short seasons.

*When to plant:* When nighttime temperatures are consistently warmer than 65°F.

*Planting and growing tips:*

- Okra is a very drought- and heat-tolerant tropical plant. Put it where it will get as much sunshine as possible all summer long.
- A relative of hibiscus, okra makes a striking, tall ornamental plant in flowerbeds or containers.

- Okra plants can reach up to five feet high or even taller, but you can contain them to about three feet by clipping off the top growth. This will result in a bushier plant.
- Harvest okra pods by clipping them off the plant rather than pulling them off with your hands. Regular picking stimulates the plant to keep producing more pods.

## ONIONS

*What to plant:* Sets, or little bulbs with green shoots on top. For fresh-eating, try sweet and mild-flavored Walla Walla. Copra keeps well for months in storage. He-Shi-Ko tolerates cool, damp soil to produce crisp scallions in spring.

*When to plant:* When the soil is dry and warmer than 50°F.

*Planting and growing tips:*

- Soggy soil causes onions to rot. Plant them where the soil is loose and well-drained—a raised bed is ideal.
- Mix in a lot of compost where you plant

onions, but otherwise refrain from fertilizing them. Too much nitrogen encourages the growth of green leaves at the expense of the bulbs.

- To produce big bulbs, plant onions at least six inches apart. If you want scallions, just two inches between each set is sufficient.

- Harvest onions after the leaves turn yellow-brown and flop over in mid to late summer.

## OREGANO

*What to plant:* Seedlings. The pink-flowered variety is more attractive and, in my experience, tends to be less aggressive than the standard type. Greek oregano is prized for its flavor.

*When to plant:* Any time after the last frost date in spring until early fall.

*Planting and growing tips:*
- There's no need to buy oregano if you know a gardener who has some. Just ask for a clump that's three or four inches in diameter and you will soon have more

than you need.
- Oregano, like other members of the mint family, spreads rapidly in the garden. Plant it where it has room to expand or contain it by growing it in a pot (you can bury the whole pot in the garden if you like).

- Harvest oregano stems and leaves any time you want some to flavor pasta sauce or other dishes. After the first frost in fall or in early spring, cut back mounds of oregano to about three inches high.

## P

## PARSLEY

*What to plant:* Seedlings. Flat-leaved or Italian parsley varieties taste to me a little fresher or brighter than the curly types.

*When to plant:* Two to three weeks before the last frost in spring.

*Planting and growing tips:*
- The parsley worm (actually a caterpillar) becomes the black swallowtail butterfly. The caterpillar may munch your parsley,

but rarely does enough damage to keep you from harvesting all you need. Leave it be and enjoy the stunning butterflies hanging around your garden in summer.

- When the plants are taller than six inches, you can begin to snip off parsley leaves as you need them. They will be quickly replenished.
- Parsley survives winter and continues growing the following spring where temperatures are not below freezing for weeks. Parsley has a two-season life cycle, so you will have to replace it at least every other year.

## PARSNIPS

*What to plant:* Seeds. All-American and Harris Model produce smooth-skinned roots that are a modest eight to ten inches long. Gladiator keeps well in storage.

*When to plant:* Late spring to early summer, so it matures around your first frost date in fall.

*Planting and growing tips:*
- Parsnips stay sweeter if you plant them where they get partial shade during the height of summer.
- Soak parsnip seeds for a few hours before planting them. Parsnip seeds are very slow to germinate—just keep the soil consistently damp and wait.
- Parsnips grow best in soil that's loose to at least a foot deep, and as free of stones and even pebbles as can be. Add compost, but avoid adding manure and other high nitrogen fertilizers to the parsnip bed. They can cause the roots to fork instead of forming one solid root.
- Begin to harvest parsnips right after the first frost in fall. Anywhere warmer than the very far North, they can stay in the ground through the winter, but be sure to harvest them before new growth starts in spring.

## PEAS

*What to plant:* Seeds. Little Marvel and Lincoln are reliable English (or shelling) peas. If you like edible pods, try Mammoth Melting Sugar (snowpea) or Sugar Snap.

*When to plant:* Six weeks before the last frost in spring.

*Planting and growing tips:*

- After planting pea seeds, keep the soil damp but not soaking—they are prone to rot in cold, wet soil.
- If you live where spring stays cool into May, you can extend your pea harvest by sowing the seeds twice or three times at two-week intervals.
- Grow peas up bamboo poles or netting hung between two poles. This keeps the vines from tangling and makes it easy for you to find the pods.
- Treating pea seeds with inoculant, a naturally occurring microbe, before planting can increase yields. You can find inoculant online and in garden centers.
- After a vine finishes producing, cut it off at the ground level rather than pulling it out. Its roots are rich in nitrogen that can feed the next crop you plant in that space.

# PEPPERS

*What to plant:* Seedlings. Ace (bell), Red Cheese (pimento) and Jimmy Nardello's (frying) produce loads of sweet peppers. For chile peppers, you can choose from mild Numex jalapeno or fiery Scotch bonnet, and many degrees of heat in between.

*When to plant:* Two weeks after the last frost in spring.

*Planting and growing tips:*

- Peppers are tropical plants and thrive on long hours of direct, hot sunshine. Avoid planting them where they will be shaded at all.
- If you buy seedlings that already have little flowers on them, pluck them off when you plant. You want the pepper to devote its energy to growing roots in your garden before it begins fruiting.
- Drought, especially at the end of summer, makes chile peppers spicier. Adjust your watering to your taste.
- For nearly all pepper varieties, green is an unripe color. (Yes, even the green peppers sold in supermarkets.) Leave

them on the plant and they will turn to red, orange or yellow, getting more flavorful and nutritious at the same time.

- You can dig and pot up pepper plants at the end of summer, trim them back and keep them in a well-lit place indoors until the following spring. They plants won't produce peppers over winter, but they will start sooner the next spring because they will already be at a mature size.

## POTATOES

*What to plant:* Seed potatoes, or chunks of full-size spuds with an eye. For the longest harvest, plant a mix that mature at different times, such as Superior (early), Yukon Gold (midseason) and King Harry (late). Gourmet fingerlings such as Russia Banana are as easy to grow as the standard types.

*When to plant:* Two to four weeks before the last frost date in spring.

*Planting and growing tips:*
- Plant certified disease-free seed potatoes to protect your crop from scab and other potential problems lurking in the soil.
- Wait to plant until the soil is dry—this is more critical than the exact timing for planting potatoes because cold, wet soil can spoil the crop. If your garden soil stays soggy well into spring, plant potatoes in a barrel (see page 41).
- An easy way to grow potatoes is to simply scatter the seed chunks on top of the soil—no digging necessary—and cover them with at least six inches of organic mulch. Whether you bury them in the soil or grow them on top of it, keep mounding mulch around the stems of the potato plants as they grow so that no light reaches the spuds and turns them green.
- New potatoes are ready to harvest about three weeks after the first flowers bloom on the plants. For heftier potatoes, wait until the top green growth dies down at the end of the season before digging them up.

## PUMPKINS

*What to plant:* Seeds. Jack-Be-Little and Baby Bear produce small pumpkins on modest- (for pumpkins) sized vines. Rouge Vif D'Etampes is a French heirloom often referred to as the Cinderella pumpkin. Small Sugar makes sweet pie filling.

*When to plant:* A week or two after the last frost date in spring.

*Planting and growing tips:*

• Pumpkin vines spread rapidly and take up a lot of room, so be sure they have space to run where you plant them. You can train the smaller-fruited types to grow up a fence or other structure, saving space in your garden.

• Plant pumpkin seeds in groups of four in a mound, or hill, or soil. The vines will spread out in all directions.

• Build up the hill with a lot of compost—pumpkins are heavy feeders.

• Pumpkins can withstand a few frosts, but they are ripe and ready for harvest as soon as they turn fully orange and the vines begin to yellow.

## R

## RADICCHIO

*What to plant:* Seeds. Look for heading varieties, such as compact Rossa di Chioggia. Radicchio di Treviso produces a more cylindrical shaped head (like Romaine lettuce).

*When to plant:* About four weeks before the last frost in spring or in late summer for fall harvest.

*Planting and growing tips:*

• If spring quickly turns to summer where you live, plant radicchio where it will get partial shade or grow it in the fall.

• About ten weeks after planting radicchio, cut off a third of its top growth (you can eat what you've lopped off). This stimulates the plant to start forming a head.

• You can harvest a few radicchio leaves as the plant is growing. The heads are ready to eat when the leaves are tightly bunched and they feel solid.

## RADISHES

*What to plant:* Seeds. Cherry Belle is the classic round red and white variety. Icicle forms long, white, spicy roots. Easter Egg blend gives you a mix of purple, red, pink and white radishes.

*When to plant:* As soon as you can work in the soil in spring and every two weeks after until early summer.

*Planting and growing tips:*

• Round radishes need loose soil only to six inches deep. Longer types grow best where the soil is loose a foot deep.

• Radishes are quick to mature—some are ready in as little as three weeks after planting. Grow them where you intend to plant hot weather crops later in the season, when the radishes are long gone.

• Harvest radishes when the top of the roots start poking through the soil surface. Don't wait too long because they crack open and become woody when they get too large.

## RHUBARB

*What to plant:* Crowns, or clumps of roots with a few short shoots. Valentine has brilliant red stems that hold their color when cooked. Linnaeus comes up earlier than most varieties and stays smaller.

*When to plant:* Anytime from early spring to late summer.

*Planting and growing tips:*

• Rhubarb is a perennial that produces its first crop a year after planting. It will keep producing for twenty more years or even longer. Each year rhubarb needs a period when temperatures stay below 40°F before it starts growing new stems.

• Plant rhubarb so that the little buds on top of the crowns are level with the soil line. You're likely to get all the rhubarb you need from two to three plants.

• Remove flower stalks the first season to direct the plants' energy into growing roots and leaf stems.

• As the plants age, they become crowded and the leaf stems get smaller. Rejuvenate your rhubarb patch by digging the roots up in fall, breaking them into smaller pieces with a shovel and then replanting the most robust-looking pieces. Give the extra root clumps to a friend who wants to grow rhubarb.

## ROSEMARY

*What to plant:* Seedlings. Arp is more cold-tolerant than other varieties. Blue Boy, named for its sky-hued flowers, stays compact so it's ideal for small plots and containers.

*When to plant:* Two weeks after the last frost date in spring.

*Planting and growing tips:*
- Rosemary grows like a small shrub (though it can get quite large where winters are mild) and opens loads of little white, pink or blue flowers in midsummer. That makes it both attractive and practical to plant it in a flowerbed or a container.
- Rosemary is so drought-tolerant you will rarely, if ever, need to water it after it is established (three to four weeks after planting).

- Getting more rosemary is easy when you have one. Just clip a shoot that's about six inches long, pluck the leaves off and plant the stem in the soil. Keep it moist and it will begin growing in a couple weeks. If winters are freezing where you live, try this in late summer, put the shoot in a pot and keep it in a sunny windowsill. You can trim off leaves and stems to eat all through winter.

## S

## SAGE

*What to plant:* Seedlings. Berggarten sage is a long-lived variety. Tricolor is the prettiest and pineapple sage is the best-tasting.

*When to plant:* A week or two after the last frost date in spring.

*Planting and growing tips:*
- Leave space between the sage seedlings and other plants so that air can circulate freely around the plant and keep fungus from forming. Bear in mind that as sage grows it sprawls.

- After sage flowers, trim off about a third of the leaves (choose the biggest and oldest) to stimulate the growth of tender new leaves.
- Sage is a perennial but in my garden in Pennsylvania, it rarely lasts longer than three or four seasons before I need to replant it.

## STRAWBERRIES

*What to plant:* Seedlings. June-bearing varieties such as Allstar produce a large harvest all at once—they're best for making pies and jam. Ever-bearing (also known as day-neutral) varieties such as Tristar yield fewer berries at a time but produce over a longer period. Alpine strawberries are tiny, very sweet and ideal for the smallest spaces and containers.

*When to plant:* Early spring, as soon as the soil is dry enough to work in.

*Planting and growing tips:*
- Avoid planting strawberries where you've recently grown tomatoes or peppers, because they are all prone to similar diseases that live in the soil.
- Mix compost into the soil to create mounds in which to plant strawberries. Set the plants so that soil just covers the roots but not the crown (where the roots meet the shoots).
- Strawberries send out "runners," or stems on top of the soil, that create new plants. If your garden does not have room for strawberries to spread out, you can plant them in a pot (see page 31 for details) or just cut off the runners to keep the mother plant producing. This works best with ever-bearing varieties.
- Protect garden-grown strawberries from rotting with a thick layer of organic mulch on the soil around them. The best mulch is (you guessed it) straw.
- Feed strawberries with compost tea or other liquid organic fertilizer after all the berries are harvested.

## SPINACH

*What to plant:* Seeds. Bloomsdale Long-standing tolerates cold temperatures, which makes it great for fall planting. Tyee withstands heat better than most varieties, so it's best for climates where spring heats up quickly. Baby's Leaf produces tender leaves with small stems.

*When to plant:* Early spring and late summer.

*Planting and growing tips:*
- Spinach turns tough and bitter when temperatures heat up. If your garden's soil is too cold and wet to work in early spring, grow spinach as a fall crop by planting it in late summer.
- Shade and constant moisture can keep spinach from turning bitter as the temperatures rise in late spring.
- You can begin eating spinach leaves when the plant has more than six leaves that are three inches long. Always leave at least three behind when you harvest to be sure the plant has the power to produce more of them.
- See page 17 for how to grow spinach over the winter in even cold climates.

# SWEET POTATOES

*What to plant:* Slips, or sprouts from chunks of the previous year's potatoes. Purple-skinned Beauregard is a heavy producer. The vines of Bush Porto Rico tend to take up less space than most other varieties.

*When to plant:* After the last frost in spring.

*Planting and growing tips:*
- Sweet potatoes are tropical plants that need 100 days or more of warm weather to fully mature. Gardeners in northern climates often use black plastic mulch to speed the warming of the soil for sweet potatoes. I generally try to keep plastic out of my organic garden, but I realize it may be the only way to grow sweet potatoes and melons in regions where the growing season is too short.
- With their bright green vines and white to purplish flowers, sweet potatoes are a good-looking choice to grow in hanging baskets and other large containers.
- To get tubers with firm texture, stop

watering your sweet potatoes about three weeks before they are ready to harvest.

- Dig underneath the roots to avoid cutting any open with your shovel. Don't wash them—just brush the dirt off—and let them "cure" for a couple weeks in a cool, dry spot away from direct sun before storing them.

*T* ▬▬▬▬▬▬▬▬▬▬

## TARRAGON

*What to plant:* Seedlings. French tarragon has the genuine peppery, vinegary flavor. Russian tarragon and Mexican tarragon are different species altogether.

*When to plant:* After the last frost in spring.

*Planting and growing tips:*
- Very loose, sandy soil is ideal for growing tarragon. If your garden's soil is heavy clay, add lots of compost to the bed before planting tarragon or plant it in a pot with plenty of peat mixed in.
- A full-size tarragon plant can reach two feet across. Leave room around each plant for air to flow through and evaporate moisture that can rot it.
- Tarragon is a perennial that typically lasts three to four years. Every other season, take a few cuttings from tarragon, plant them in small pots with a light soil mix, and keep them moist until they start to grow. This will continually renew your tarragon supply.

## THYME

*What to plant:* Seedlings. French thyme has the most delicate flavor. Lemon thyme has a fresh fragrance, though no citrus flavor when cooked.

*When to plant:* After the last frost in spring.

*Planting and growing tips:*
- Though it is a member of the mint family, thyme is a slow-grower. It also grows low to the ground, making it useful to fill spaces in flowerbeds and attractive

spilling over ledges and other obstacles in rock gardens.

- Prune thyme regularly—every other week during the growing season, if possible—to stimulate new growth and keep the stems from becoming woody. Eat the prunings or dry them to use later.
- Dried thyme is three times more flavorful than fresh.

## TOMATILLO

*What to plant:* Seedlings. Toma Verde grows well in a wide variety of conditions and yields big, juicy fruit.

*When to plant:* When nighttime temperatures are consistently warmer than 60°F.

*Planting and growing tips:*
- No surprise for a plant native to Mexico—tomatillos are very heat and drought tolerant, but very sensitive to cold. Plant them in your garden's hottest spot.
- You need two tomatillo plants to get thorough pollination and a healthy yield of little fruit.

- Harvest tomatillos when they almost fill the husk—about walnut size. The fruit at the bottom of the plant ripens first. If you leave them on the vine too long, the bright citrusy flavor starts to sour.

## TOMATOES

*What to plant:* Seedlings. Large beefsteak varieties, such as Big Beef and heirloom Cherokee Purple, taste best. Cherry tomatoes, such as Sweet Million and Sungold are the most productive. San Marzano is a great-tasting and productive paste type tomato. Bush, or determinate, varieties grow to a size manageable in a container.

*When to plant:* After the last frost in spring.

*Planting and growing tips:*
- Tomato plants yield the most fruit when they get ten or more hours of sunlight each day in summer.
- Dig deep planting holes or trenches so that you can bury tomatoes' stems all the way up to the lowest set of leaves. New roots will grow on the buried stem—

more roots mean a bigger, sturdier, more productive plant.

- Pluck off any flowers on tomato seedlings when you plant them so that all their energy goes first into building roots before it starts setting fruit.
- Caged tomato plants yield more than staked ones, but the fruit isn't as easy to access.
- Feed tomato plants with compost tea or other liquid organic fertilizer every other week until they start flowering—then stop.
- If you let tomatoes fall to the ground in your garden, you will be pulling out many seedlings the following summer.

## TURNIPS

*What to plant:* Seeds. Purple Top White Globe produces tender, four-to five-inch roots. Tokyo Cross matures just a month after planting. Seven Top, an heirloom, grows lush, tasty greens on top.

*When to plant:* As soon as the soil dries out in spring.

*Planting and growing tips:*
- Turnips are a close relative of cabbage, broccoli and other members of the brassica family. Avoid planting turnips in soil where you have grown any of them in the past three years.
- Planting a new row of turnip seeds every two weeks from early spring to early summer gives you a steady supply of greens and roots to enjoy all season long.
- You can start harvesting and eating turnip greens when the plant has more than six leaves. Be sure to leave a few behind to support the still-growing roots. The roots taste less bitter after a frost.

W▬▬▬▬▬▬▬▬▬▬

## WATERMELON

*What to plant:* Seeds. Moon and Stars is a super sweet and juicy heirloom. Bush Sugar Baby bears modest, 12-pound fruit on vines that are shorter (under four feet) than other varieties. Rainbow Sherbet is a mix of red, yellow and orange fleshed varieties that mature in less than the standard ninety days.

*When to plant:* Two weeks after the last frost in spring.

*Planting and growing tips:*
- Plant seeds in groups of six with two to three feet between clusters. After the seeds sprout and have four or more leaves, pull out the three least vigorous-looking plants.
- Watermelons need lots of water—consistent moisture is ideal—to fill out completely and reach their full potential. Water them deeply once a week and keep a solid layer of mulch around them.
- To keep soil-dwelling pests from damaging the fruits, put a piece of wood or burlap underneath each melon as it ripens.
- There are many tricks you hear about for telling when a watermelon is at its peak of ripeness. I can say for sure that every ripe watermelon has a pale yellow patch somewhere on its skin.

# WINTER SQUASH

*What to plant:* Seeds. Bush varieties of acorn, butternut, hubbard and spaghetti squash grow more compact vines than standard types. Delicata doesn't store as well as the others, but it has exceptionally tender flesh and a very sweet flavor.

*When to plant:* Two weeks after the last frost in spring.

*Planting and growing tips:*
- When you water winter squash, try to direct it straight to the roots rather than the leaves, which are prone to fungal diseases. If mildew blooms on your winter squash, use the baking soda solution on page 56 to treat it.
- Squash depend on insects for pollination. Attract pollinators by planting squash in an area where herbs and flowers are growing.
- By midsummer, winter squash will have set all the fruit it can mature before the season ends. Remove any new flowers that form after that to direct the plants' energy into ripening the fruit it already has.

- Winter squash are ready to harvest when the area where the vine meets the fruit begins to turn brown.

Z ▓▓▓▓▓▓▓▓▓▓▓▓▓▓▓

## ZUCCHINI AND SUMMER SQUASH

*What to plant:* Seeds. Gold Rush and Yellow Crookneck bear loads of tender, evenly shaped fruit. Peter Pan is a productive round summer squash.

*When to plant:* Two weeks after the last frost.

*Planting and growing tips:*

- Two summer squash vines will ensure adequate pollination for the plants and plenty of the vegetables for you to harvest.
- Save space and create natural shade for other crops by growing summer squash on a vertical support of some kind. See page 21 for how to set up a bamboo trellis.
- Pick zucchini and summer squash when they are less than six inches long—any bigger and they start to become woodier and seedier. You can avoid damaging the vine when you harvest by clipping rather than pulling the squash off.

# RESOURCES

**I**n this book I've tried to introduce you to the basic skills of homesteading, give you enough information to get started, and share hints and tricks that will help you apply the skills to city-size properties. I hope I have inspired you to try some of these skills yourself, and once you do, you will discover there is so much more to learn on each of these topics than I could fit into this book. Encyclopedic books and vast online archives have been compiled on every one of these topics. Through blogs, online forums, and social media, homesteaders around the world are sharing their real-world experiences.

There's no shortage of information, anecdote, and opinion; here are a few reliable places to help you dig deeper into each of the subjects. You will see that I have a preference for universities, government, and established nonprofits as sources of information. I've also included here some suppliers of the products and gear you might use in your garden or around your homestead. Just to be upfront: I have no financial relationship with any of these sources and recommend them solely based on my own experience with them and their commitment to organic or eco-friendly practices.

## GROWING INFORMATION

Every state has a "land-grant" university that is charged with collecting information on gardening—as well as composting, food preservation, beekeeping, and other homesteading topics—and sharing it with the public through their cooperative extension service. In most states they also train "master gardeners," who respond to questions from the public via e-mail or on the telephone. Most counties have a cooperative extension office—find yours and you'll discover an invaluable resource of information about your region.

Many of the nation's leading land-grant universities share their vast archives of gardening information online. I've listed a few of the deepest and most useful Web sites for different parts of the United States.

### CORNELL UNIVERSITY
**www.gardening.cornell.edu**

### OHIO STATE UNIVERSITY
**http://webgarden.osu.edu**

### UNIVERSITY OF CALIFORNIA AT DAVIS
**http://ucanr.org/sites/gardenweb**

### UNIVERSITY OF FLORIDA
**http://solutionsforyourlife.ufl.edu/lawn_and_garden**

***How to Grow More Vegetables Than You Ever Thought Possible on Less Land Than You Can Imagine,*** by John Jeavons (Ten Speed Press, 1979)
A detailed explanation of the bio-intensive planting method that helps you to boost your harvest while building soil fertility and conserving water.

***The Organic Gardener's Handbook of Natural Pest and Disease Control***, by Fern Marshall Bradley, Barbara W. Ellis, and Deborah L. Martin (Rodale, 2010)
The easiest-to-use manual for solving all sorts of garden problems without toxic chemicals.

***Rodale's Ultimate Encyclopedia of Organic Gardening***, edited by Fern Marshall Bradley, Barbara W. Ellis, and Ellen Phillips (Rodale, 2009)
The standard reference book has recently been updated, with in-depth entries on every topic from alliums to zinc.

***Square Foot Gardening***, by Mel Bartholomew (Rodale, 2005)
If you like a systematic approach, this is your guidebook to using your space efficiently.

***Uncommon Fruits for Every Garden***, by Lee Reich, Ph.D. (Timber Press, 2008)
This book introduces you to edible fruits that you don't find in grocery stores, but are suited to urban and suburban yards.

***The Vegetable Gardener's Bible***, by Edward C. Smith (Storey Books, 2009)
An A-to-Z guide to growing every crop with a focus on maximizing the yields.

## SEEDS, PLANTS, AND SUPPLIES

Organic seeds are now more widely available than ever and even some of the biggest, oldest companies now offer some seeds that have not been treated with fungicides and other chemicals. The following seed sources not only offer organic seeds, they specialize in heirloom varieties or those that are well-adapted to particular regions.

Before you buy seeds or transplants, check out ratings of hundreds of vegetable varieties submitted by gardeners from around the country based on their own experience with them at Vegetable Varieties for Gardeners, operated by Cornell University: **http://vegvariety.cce.cornell.edu/.**

### BAKER CREEK HEIRLOOM SEEDS

A great source of information and inspiration
as well as an extensive selection of classic varieties.

**www.rareseeds.com**

### GARDENER'S SUPPLY CO.

Containers of all types and shapes, rain barrels,
season-extension, trellises, and other gardening aids.

**www.gardeners.com**

### GARDENS ALIVE!

Organic fertilizers and nontoxic pest control products.

**www.gardensalive.com**

### GARDENWEB

The Internet's most active online forum for gardeners with dedicated chat rooms for organic growing, swapping seeds, and more specific subjects, such as heirloom varieties and vertical gardens.

**www.gardenweb.com**

## JOHNNY'S SELECTED SEEDS

Specializes in varieties suited to cold climates and
offers help extending the growing season.

**www.johnnyseeds.com**

## PEACEFUL VALLEY FARM & GARDEN SUPPLY

Potted fruit trees, seed potatoes, garlic for planting, and a variety of seeds,
sprouting equipment, cheesemaking kits, and more homesteading supplies.

**www.groworganic.com**

## PLANET NATURAL

The widest selection of organic pest control products for garden and home.

**www.planetnatural.com**

## SEED SAVERS EXCHANGE

You can buy seeds or become a member to preserve and swap rare varieties with other
members.

**www.seedsavers.org**

## SEEDS OF CHANGE

All organic seeds, many heirlooms, and other unique varieties.

**www.seedsofchange.comTerritorial**

A wide selection of organic seeds and plants.

**www.territorialseed.com**

### DR. DUKE'S GREEN PHARMACY

James A. Duke, Ph.D., is a renowned botanist and USDA researcher who now focuses his studies on foraged plants for eating and healing.
**www.greenpharmacy.com**

### FORAGING WITH "WILDMAN" STEVE BRILL

He may be a "wild and crazy guy," but Brill shares just about everything you need to know about finding, gathering and eating wild plants.
**www.wildmanstevebrill.com/**

### NORTH AMERICAN MYCOLOGICAL ASSOCIATION

Maintains a state-by-state listing of mushroom-hunting clubs while supporting fungi science and the preservation of natural habitat.
**www.namyco.org**

***The Forager's Harvest,*** by Samuel Thayer (Forager's Harvest Press, 2006)
The most useful wild plant guide because the author focuses only on those plants that taste good rather than those that are merely edible.

***North American Mushrooms***, by Dr. Orson K. Miller Jr. and Hope Miller (Falcon, 2006)
Big photographs and clear descriptions help you make that all-important positive identification.

***Stalking the Wild Asparagus***, by Euell Gibbons (Alan C. Hood & Co., 2005)
A classic book full of detailed information on foraging and ideas for how to prepare and serve wild foods at home.

### CANNING ACROSS AMERICA

A nonprofit that's devoted to the "lost art of putting up food." The Web site lists canning classes and events, and offers recipes from well-known chefs. Its user-submitted photos will have you checking back often for fresh inspiration.

**www.canningacrossamerica.com**

### KITCHEN KRAFTS

Complete selection of supplies for canning, dehydrating, pickling, and more.

**www.kitchenkrafts.com**

### NATIONAL CENTER FOR HOME FOOD PRESERVATION

Comprehensive information from the U.S. Department of Agriculture on every aspect of home food preservation, and critical details on processing times for canners, with links to many other valuable university sites.

**www.uga.edu/nchfp**

***Ball Complete Book of Home Preserving*** by Judi Kingry and
  Lauren Devine (Robert Rose, 2006)

I wouldn't ordinarily recommend a book produced by a manufacturing company, but Ball has been the leading purveyor of canning supplies for more than a hundred years. This book is like a founding document home-steaders have been using since the 1880s, except that it's in a paperback full of tested recipes especially handy for beginning canners. You can also order Ball canning supplies directly from the company's Web site.

www.freshpreserving.com

# Backyard Livestock

### AMERICAN LIVESTOCK BREEDS CONSERVANCY

A nonprofit dedicated to preserving traditional breeds and the genetic diversity of working animals. The classifieds and resources section of the Web site are very helpful when you're ready to get animals of your own. **http://albc-usa.org**

### AMERICAN RABBIT BREEDERS ASSOCIATION

Most of this organization's attention is on showing rabbits, but even if that's not your goal, you can find reputable breeders to get rabbits from on the Web site's searchable listings.
**www.arba.net**

### BEE CULTURE

A magazine about beekeeping, professional and amateur. Its Web site hosts a deep reservoir of articles, including information about beekeeping in populated areas and state-by-state listings of beekeeping associations.
**www.beeculture.com**

### THE GOAT JUSTICE LEAGUE

The name alone is reason enough to check out this nonprofit organization, but when you get to its Web site, you'll find lots of valuable details presented in a practical, friendly voice on raising goats in urban and suburban environments, including the legal and zoning issues. Just check out the photos.
**www.goatjusticeleague.org**

## POULTRY BREEDS FROM THE OKLAHOMA STATE UNIVERSITY DEPARTMENT OF ANIMAL SCIENCE

Pictures and detailed descriptions of the most common, useful breeds of chicken, ducks, geese, and other fowl.

**http://139.78.104.1/breeds/poultry/**

***The Backyard Beekeeper,*** by Kim Flottum (Quarry, Rev. ed. 2010)
   A beginner's guide that's loaded with information about caring for the bees and harvesting the honey, with lots of big, beautiful, and helpful photos.

***Barnyard in Your Backyard***, by Gail Damerow (Storey, 2002)
   The details you need for raising ducks, geese, rabbits, and goats—sheep and cattle, too, if you have the space.

***Chickens in Your Backyard***, by Rick and Gail Luttman (Rodale, 1976)
   All the practical information you need for raising a small flock the natural way, told with knowing humor.

## COMMON SENSE PEST CONTROL

This site, by the Bio-Integral Resource Center, is the most comprehensive and practical guide to dealing with pests of home and garden, with an emphasis on the least toxic solutions. At the Web site you can purchase low-cost "bulletins" on proven methods of eradicating urban pests, including head lice, fleas, and rats.

**www.birc.org**

## GREEN CULTURE

The most comprehensive selection of composting bin designs, as well as rain barrels, aids for extending the gardening season, and human-powered lawn mowers.

**www.composters.com**

## THE LAUNDRY ALTERNATIVE

Portable, hand-powered washing machines and dryers.

**www.laundry-alternative.com**

## LEHMAN'S

Hand-powered appliances, food mills, and other new and old-fashioned products that help make your household more self-sufficient.

**www.lehmans.com**

*Whole Green Catalog*, edited by Michael W. Robbins (Rodale, 2009)
   A compendium of ideas, products, and services for eco-conscious living, organized in categories ranging from home-building and renovating to housekeeping and pet care.

# BIBLIOGRAPHY

*American Livestock Breeds Conservancy.* http://www.albc-usa.org.

Bartholomew, Mel. *Square Foot Gardening.* Reissue. Emmaus, PA: Rodale Press Books, 2005.

Belanger, Jerome D. *Raising Goats the Modern Way.* Pownal, VT: Storey Communications, 1990.

Bennett, Bob. *Raising Rabbits the Modern Way.* Pownal, VT: Storey Communications, 1988.

Bennett, Pamela J. "Growing Beets in the Home Garden." *Horticulture Series Factsheet.* Ohio State University. http://www.ohioline.osu.edu/hyg-fact/1000/index.html

—————"Growing Carrots in the Home Garden." *Horticulture Series Factsheet.* Ohio State University. http://www.ohioline.osu.edu/hyg-fact/1000/index.html.

—————."Growing Cucumbers in the Home Garden." *Horticulture Series Factsheet.* Ohio State University. http://www.ohioline.osu.edu/hyg-fact/1000/index.html.

Bone, Eugenia. *Well-Preserved: Recipes and techniques for putting up small batches of seasonal foods.* New York: Clarkson Potter, 2009.

Bradley, Fern Marshall, Barbara Ellis and Ellen Phillips, editors. *Rodale's Ultimate Encyclopedia of Organic Gardening.* Emmaus, PA: Rodale Press Books, 2009.

Brown, Maurus. "Basic Principles of Pruning Backyard Grapevines." *Horticulture Series Factsheet.* Ohio State University. http://www.ohioline.osu.edu/hyg-fact/1000/index.html.

Burns, Deborah. *Storey's Basic Country Skills: A Practical Guide to Self-Reliance.* Pownal, VT: Storey Communications, 1999.

*Canning Across America.* http://canningacrossamerica.com.

Cantaluppi, Carl J. "Growing Asparagus in the Home Garden." *Horticulture Series Factsheet.* Ohio State University. http://www.ohioline.osu.edu/hyg-fact/1000/index.html.

Chadwick, Janet. *The Busy Person's Guide to Preserving Food.* Pownal, VT: Storey Communications, 1995.

*Cheesemaking at Home: The Complete Illustrated Guide.* New York: Doubleday, 1974.

Damerow, Gail. *Storey's Guide to Raising Chickens.* Pownal, VT: Storey Books, 1995.

Damerow Gail, Nancy Searle and Darrell L. Salisbury. *Barnyard in Your Backyard: A beginner's guide to raising chickens, ducks, geese, rabbits, goats, sheep and cattle.* Pownal, VT: Storey Books, 2002.

"Drying Food." University of Illinois Urbana-Champaign. http://aces.uiuc.edu/vista/html_pubs/DRYING/dryfood.html.

Duke, James A. *Dr. Duke's Green Pharmacy*. http://www.greenpharmacy.com.

Flottum, Kim. *The Backyard Beekeeper: An Absolute Beginner's Guide to Keeping Bees in Your Yard*. Beverly, MA: Quarry Books, 2010.

"Foraging with Wildman Steve Brill." http://www.wildmanstevebrill.com.

*GardenWeb*. iVillage. http://www.gardenweb.com.

Gastier, Ted. "Growing Muskmelons in the Home Garden." *Horticulture Series Factsheet*. Ohio State University. http://www.ohioline.osu.edu/hyg-fact/1000/index.html.

*The Goat Justice League*. http://www.goatjusticeleague.org.

Greene, Janet C. *Putting Food By*. Brattleboro: Stephen Greene, 1988.

Haegele, Katie. "Geonoshing." *The Philadelphia Inquirer* 5 Aug 2010: F1, F4.

Haynes, Cythnia. *Raising Turkeys, Ducks, Geese, Pigeons and Guineas*. Blue Ridge Summit, PA: TAB Books, 1987.

*Homesteading Today*. http:/www.homesteadingtoday.com.

*How to Homestead*. University of San Francisco. http://www.howtohomestead.org.

Hupping, Carol. *Stocking Up III: The All-New Edition of America*, 3rd ed. Emmaus, PA: Rodale Press Books, 1986.

Jeavons, John. *How to Grow More Vegetables than You Ever Thought Possible on Less Land Than You Can Imagine*. 7th ed. Berkeley: Ten Speed, 2006.

Kilarski, Barbara. "New Chicks on the Block." *Hobby Farms Magazine: Urban Farm Sustainable City Living* Summer 2010: 34-37.

Kivirist, Lisa. "When Life Gives You Lemons, Give Back." *Hobby Farms Magazine: Urban Farm Sustainable City Living* Summer 2010: 28-31.

*La Vida Locavore*. http:/www.lavidalocavore.org.

Life Unplugged. http:/www.lifeunplugged.net.

Lyle, Katie Letcher. *The Complete Guide to Edible Wild Plants, Mushrooms, Fruits, How to Find, Identify and Cook Them*. Guilford, CT: Lyons Press, 2004.

Luttman, Rick and Gail. *Chickens in Your Backyard: A Beginner's Guide*. Emmaus, PA: Rodale Press Books, 1976.

Morrison, Cheryl. "Small-Space Storage Solutions." *Hobby Farms Magazine: Urban Farm Sustainable City Living* Summer 2010: 86-91.

Mother Earth News. Ogden Publications Inc. http://motherearthnews.com.

*National Center for Home Food Preservation*. The University of Georgia. http://uga.edu/nchfp.

*Natural Insect Control*. Brooklyn, NY: Brooklyn Botanic Garden Inc., 1994.

Nearing, Helen. *Continuing the Good Life, Half a Century of Homesteading*. New York: Schocken Books, 1979.

Nick, Jean M.A. and Fern Marshall Bradley, editors. *Growing Fruits and Vegetables Organically*. Emmaus, PA: Rodale Press Books, 1994.

Olkowski, William, Sheila Daar and Helga Olkowski. *Common-Sense Pest Control*. Newtown, CT: Taunton Press, 1991.

Prowse, Brad. *Jerkymaking for the Home, Trail and Campfire*. Happy Camp, CA: Naturegraph Publishers, 1995. Print.

"Poultry Breeds." Oklahoma State University, Department of Animal Science. http://139.78.104.1/breeds/poultry/.

Reich, Lee. *Uncommon Fruits for Every Garden*. Portland, OR: Timber Press, 2008.

Riofrio, Marianne. "Growing Broccoli and Cauliflower in the Home Garden." *Horticulture Series Factsheet*. Ohio State University. http://www.ohioline.osu.edu/hyg-fact/1000/index.html.

Ruppenthal, R.J. *Fresh Food from Small Spaces: The Square-Inch Gardener's Guide to Year-Round Growing, Fermenting and Sprouting*. White River Junction, VT: Chelsea Green Publishing, 2008.

Seymour, John. *The Self-Sufficient Life and How to Live It: The Complete Back to Basics Guide*. London: DK Publishing, 2009.

Smith, Edward C. *The Vegetable Gardener's Bible*. 2nd edition. Pownal, VT: Storey Books, 2000.

Smith, Virginia A. "21st-Century Homesteading." *The Philadelphia Inquirer* 15 Aug 2010: A1, A10.

Thayer, Samuel. *Forager's Harvest*. 2nd ed. Cleveland, NY: The Forager Press, 2006.

Thomas, Steven. *Backyard Livestock*. Woodstock, VT: The Countryman Press, 1990.

*Vegetable Varieties for Gardeners*. Cornell University. http://vegvariety.cce.cornell.edu.

Vivian, John. *Manual of Practical Homesteading*. Emmaus, PA: Rodale Press Books, 1975.

Waller, Sharon Biggs. "Barnyard in your Backyard." *Hobby Farms Magazine: Urban Farm Sustainable City Living* Summer 2010: 38-43.

# INDEX